Adobe
Photoshop
for Beginners

Adobe Photoshop for Beginners

A Complete Beginners to Pro Illustrated Guide to Learn and Master the Latest Adobe Photoshop Features and Functions With Tips and Tricks for Photoshop Users

KENT PETERSON

Adobe Photoshop for Beginners

Copyright © 2021 by Kent Peterson

All Rights Reserved.
No part of this book may be reproduced, stored in a retrievable system, transmitted in any form, or by any means, electronic, mechanical, photocopying, recording, or otherwise, without prior written permission from the author.

contents

Introduction	9
Chapter 1: Navigating the Home Screen	**13**
How to Make Photoshop Your Windows Default Image Editor	15
Photoshop Toolbox	20
Photoshop Marquee Select Tools	21
Lasso Tools in Photoshop	22
Eraser Tool in Photoshop	24
Clone Stamp Tool in Photoshop	26
Photoshop Paint Bucket Tool	28
Magic Wand Tool	30
Chapter 2: How to Open Files	**33**
Open Files	33
How to Save Your Work	37
What Is the Best Way to Undo a Command?	41
Chapter 3: Spot Healing Tool	**45**
How to Use the Brush Tool	52
Erasing Tool	52
Magic Wand Tool	53
How to Work With Layers and the Magic Wand Tool	55

Chapter 4: Adobe Photoshop Toolbox	59
Cropping Tool	60
Clone Stamp Tool	61
Lightroom vs. Photoshop	62
When Should I Use Lightroom?	62
What Can You Do Using Lightroom?	63
Photoshop	64
What Is a RAW File?	66
Creating a Collaborative Album and Asking Others to Participate	67
Chapter 5: How Can I Export My Photos?	73
Filters	75
How to Use Smart Filters to Blur a Picture	77
Chapter 6: How to Use a Layer Mask to Substitute a Background Picture	81
How to Use a Layer Mask to Add an Item to a Picture	82
What Is the Best Way to Make a Graphic Shape in Adobe Photoshop?	84
What is the Best Way to Add Texture to a Photograph?	86
Chapter 7: How to Create a Custom Shape That Is Already Built-in in Adobe Photoshop	89
Text	90
Chapter 8: Color	95
What Is the Best Way to Choose a Color?	96
How to Work With Brushes	99
How Do You Fine-tune a Selection in Adobe Photoshop	99

Chapter 9: How Can I Get Rid of Large Objects? 101
    How to Remove Small Objects 102
    How Can I Change the Saturation and Hue? 103

Chapter 10: Selection Basics 105
    How to Work With Lasso Tools 107
    Quick Selection: How to Use It 108
    How to Flip an Image in Photoshop to Get the Mirror Image of Any Photo 109

Chapter 11: How to Unlock the Background Layer 113
    How Can I Alter the Brightness of a Color? 114
    What Is the Significance of Layers? 115
    How to Alter the Size of a Layer 116

Chapter 12: How to Include Pictures into a Layer Design 119
    How Can I Adjust the Contrast and Brightness? 120
    How Do I Make a Resolution? 122
    How to Crop and Straighten a Picture 124

Chapter 13: How Can I Change the Size of the Canvas? 127
    Tips and Tricks to Using Adobe Photoshop 129
    Choose Colors from Anywhere 130
    Install Custom Photoshop Brushes 131
    What Is the Best Way to Make a Rain Texture? 132
    Create a Light Bleed Effect in a Flash 133
    Use Blend If 134
    How to Quickly Copy Layer Styles 134
    How to Make Text Have Multiple Stroke Effects 135
    Learn How to Use Keyboard Shortcuts 136
    Learn to Merge Shapes 137
    Make Destructive Changes to New Layers At All Times 137
    Experiment With Layer Masks 139

Find Out What Works Best for You and Stick to It	140
Using Photoshop to Warp Text	140
How to Create a Photoshop Frequency Separation Action	141
How to Make a Smart Object	142
Photoshop Brushes: How to Make One	142

Conclusion 143

introduction

Back in February of 1990, when Photoshop was originally released, it made quite a stir in the creative world. Designers and photographers were able to conduct picture editing chores for the first time without turning to high-end equipment that cost twice as much. It sparked a movement that is still going on today. There have been a number of incidents throughout the years.

Adobe Photoshop is a picture editing software that allows you to create, edit, and modify a variety of images and graphics. It also allows you to generate and edit raster pictures with many layers, as well as import the images into other file formats.

This program is compatible with both macOS and Windows and may be used to modify and create new pictures. When it comes to utilizing this tool, graphic designers and photographers are at the forefront.

When you first start studying Adobe Photoshop, you'll see that there are a lot of different ways to accomplish things. The desire to constantly alter pictures is strong, particularly among photographers who are paid to capture and edit images. Imagine a period or a situation when you couldn't edit pictures with numerous flaws or scratches. Will it be a pleasant experience? Definitely not.

With the advent of Adobe Photoshop, editing has gotten simpler as the world changes and develops rapidly in terms of technology. You may always open your Adobe software and modify the recorded photos to your liking instead of constantly retaking shots with your camera.

It's entirely up to you how you use the tools that are available to you, whether it's a keyboard shortcut, right clicking, menus, or icons. In reality, even a well-taken

Introduction

photograph may be improved upon. This comprehensive user guide is a must-have for anybody seeking to get the most out of Adobe Photoshop or better grasp how it works.

ONE

Navigating the Home Screen

The following choices are available from the Home screen:

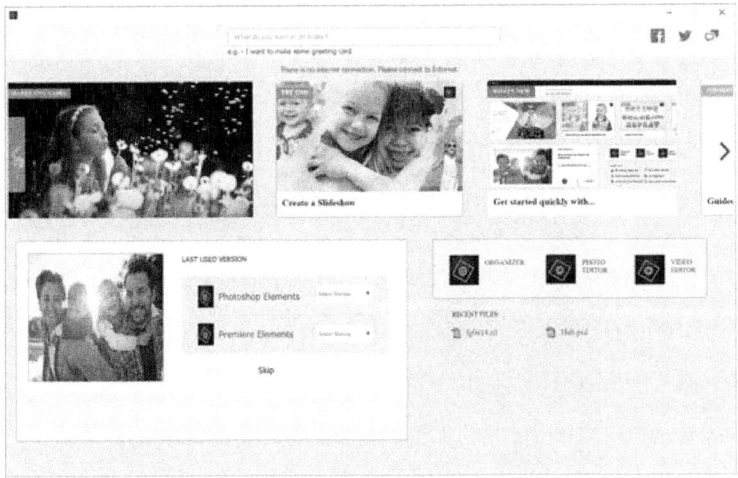

Search: You may search for a task at the top of the window and have assistance returned to you.

What's New: Click a thumbnail that displays a What's New banner to see the current release's new features.

Create a Slide Show: Selecting this option opens the Elements Organizer, which allows you to choose pictures for a slideshow.

Guided edit: The thumbnails with the Try button have been guided through the editing process. This banner provides a shortcut to the Photo Editor's Guided Edits.

Right pointing chevron (>): Click the right chevron to get a variety of sharing and creating options.

Adding More Images/Videos: To add additional pictures to the Organizer, click the icon.

Application Launcher: To open the Elements Photo Editor, the Organizer, or Adobe Premiere Elements, click one of the three icons (Premier Elements must be installed to launch this item.).

Navigating the Home Screen

Recent Files: Select a picture from the list of recent files to open it in the Photo Editor.

How to Make Photoshop Your Windows Default Image Editor

On a Windows PC, here's how to make Photoshop your default picture editor.

1. **Go to a picture on your computer**

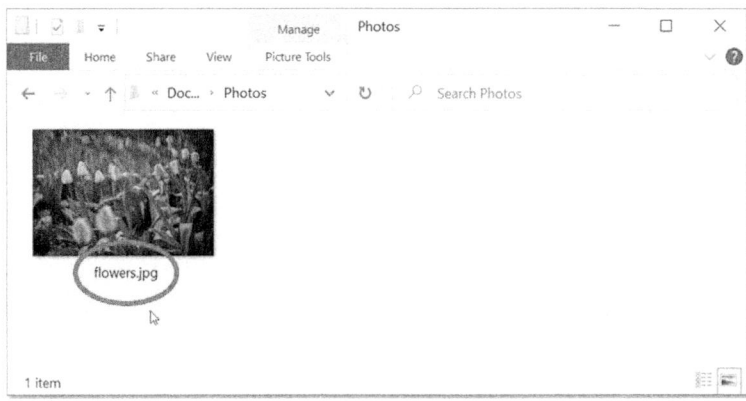

- To begin, open File Explorer on Windows and browse to a folder that contains one of your pictures. I'll use a JPEG picture, but the same procedures may be applied to other file formats such as PNG and TIFF.

Adobe Photoshop for Beginners

- The .jpg suffix following the file name tells us we're looking at a JPEG image:

How can I enable file extensions?

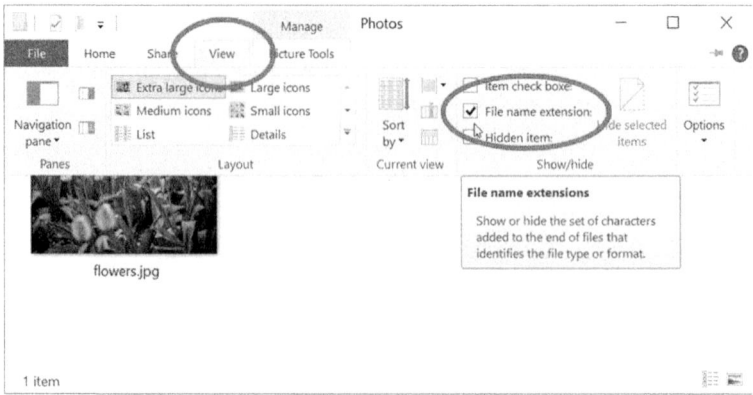

- If the file extension isn't visible, go to the View menu and choose File name extension:
- Windows comes with a built-in picture editor.
- When we double-click on a JPEG picture in Windows, the following happens by default.
- The picture loads in the Photos app, which isn't Photoshop and isn't what we're looking for.
- Close the Photos app by tapping the X in the upper right corner if this happens.

Navigating the Home Screen

2. **Select Properties from the context menu when you right-click on the picture thumbnail.**

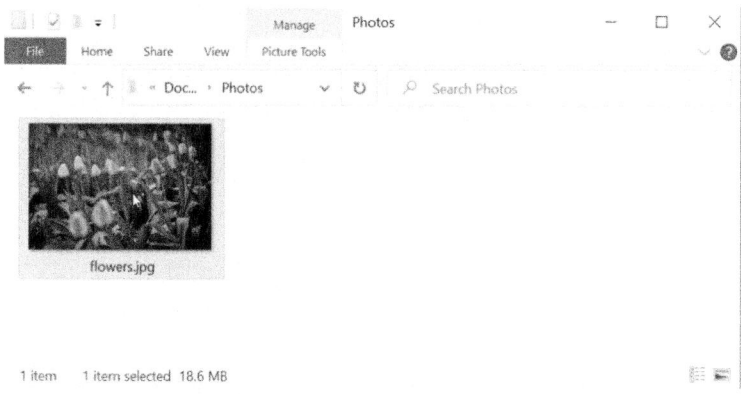

- Right-click on the picture thumbnail to have Windows open all JPEG images in Photoshop.
- And then, at the bottom of the menu, choose Properties:

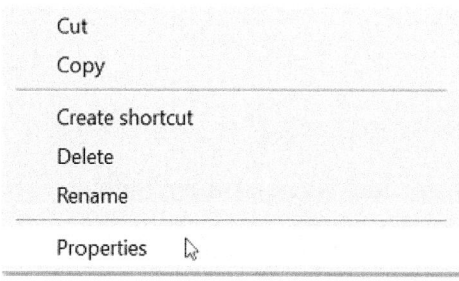

Adobe Photoshop for Beginners

3. **Select Photoshop from the Change menu**

Notice that JPEG files are presently configured to open with Photos in the Properties dialog box.

Click the Change option to make Photoshop the default image editor for JPEG files instead of Photos:

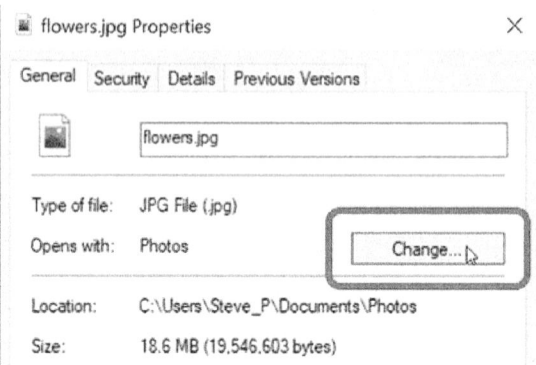

Then, on your computer, choose the most current version of Photoshop. The most recent version is Photoshop 2021:

Navigating the Home Screen

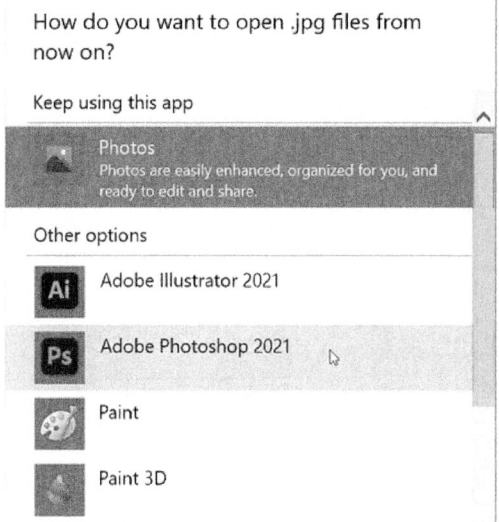

- If Photoshop isn't displayed, go to the bottom of the page and choose More Apps:
- If Photoshop isn't in the initial list, go to More Apps.
- Photoshop should also show. To pick it, click on it and then click OK:

4. **Finish by closing the Properties window.**

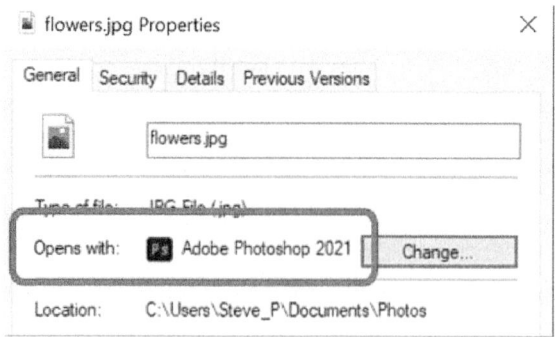

- Photoshop is now configured as the default image editor for JPEG files in the Properties dialog box.
- To exit the dialog window, click OK.
- And the picture will open in Photoshop right away. To make Photoshop your default editor for additional file formats like PNG and TIFF, just repeat these instructions.

Photoshop Toolbox

The primary tools for dealing with pictures are housed in the toolbox. To choose and utilize a tool, just click it. The presence of a tiny arrow next to a tool in the toolbox shows that it offers more choices. Click and hold your mouse on a tool in Photoshop to view its

Navigating the Home Screen

options. If you click and hold on the choose tool, for example, you'll see select choices like eliptical selection, single row selection, and so on.

Photoshop Marquee Select Tools

You may use the marquee tools to pick rectangles, ellipses, and 1-pixel rows and columns. The marquee tools are found in the Photoshop Toolbox's upper left corner. To view the four choices, click and hold your cursor on the marquee tool:

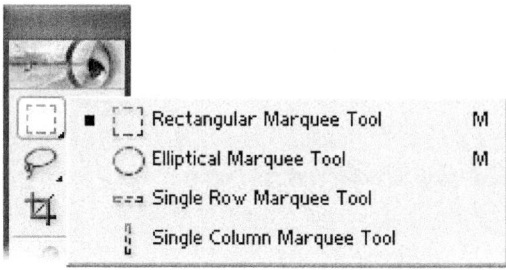

- **Rectangle Shape Marquee:** Make a rectangle selection using your mouse. Hold down the shift key to make the selection a square.
- **Elliptical** is a kind of marquee that is used to select the elliptical option. Hold down the shift key to make the selection a circle.

21

Adobe Photoshop for Beginners

- **Single row Marquee:** Make a 1 pixel high horizontal selection.
- **Single Column Marquee:** Make a 1 pixel wide vertical selection.
- **Options for a Marquee:** When you choose a marquee tool, the Tool Choices bar displays associated options (just below the main menu). This enables you to customize the selection type, feathering, and other features. Each marquee tool has somewhat different options.

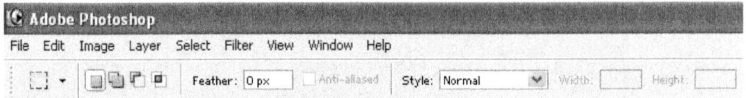

Lasso Tools in Photoshop

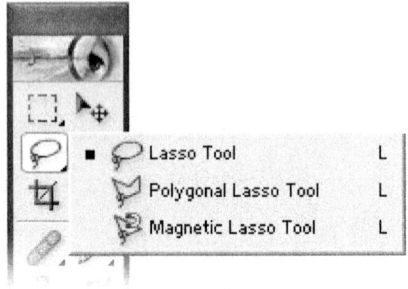

By drawing or tracing the selection outline, you may pick exact portions of a picture using the lasso tools. There are three lasso tools to choose from:

Lasso Tool

This is a tool for making freehand selections. Draw your selection by clicking and holding the left mouse button on the picture.

Lasso Tool with Polygons

Instead of holding down the mouse button to draw, left-click on different locations to make a selection with a sequence of straight edges, similar to the lasso tool.

To draw freehand parts, hold down the Alt key (Windows) or the Option key (Mac OS).

Lasso Tool with Magnets

This is a very useful tool for choosing regions with well-defined boundaries. Simply place a left-click at the start of your selection and drag the mouse down the edge.

At different places around the edges, "fastening points" are automatically created. At any moment, left-click to manually add a fastening point.

To finish a selection

To complete a selection, double-click anywhere or click on the selection's starting point.

Eraser Tool in Photoshop

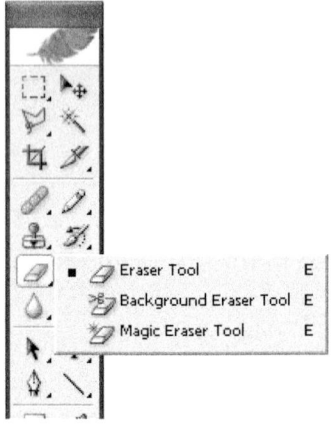

The eraser tool in Photoshop may be found in the toolbox's second set of icons. Eraser, Background Eraser, and Magic Eraser are the three variants.

The eraser is a brush that removes pixels from a picture as you drag it over it. If the layer is locked, pixels are wiped to transparency or the background color.

You have many choices in the toolbar when you choose the eraser tool:

Brush: The size of the eraser, the toughness of the edges, and other designs are all options. In block mode, there are no brush choices.

Flow: Controls the speed at which the erase is applied by the brush. The impact is more modest at lower levels. Brush mode is the only way to use it.

Mode: Brush (soft edges), pencil (hard edges), and block are the three modes available (square brush size).

Airbrush: The eraser may be used as an airbrush. Brush mode is the only way to use it.

Opacity: 100% opacity fully erases pixels, whereas 0% opacity does not delete at all. Half of it is semi-transparent.

Erase to History: Returns the picture to a previously stored state or snapshot. To utilize this functionality, go to the history palette and click the left column next to the chosen state.

Eraser Tool for the Background

The background eraser tool lets you remove the color from an image or layer's backdrop. When you click the picture, the eraser takes a sample of the color in the brush's center and erases it as you drag. You may choose the kind of erasing, color tolerance, and sample technique from the toolbar's options.

Tool for Magic Erasing

Within a certain tolerance, the magic eraser tool erases all colors. This is basically the same as pressing Delete with the magic wand. You don't have to drag with this tool; just click once.

Clone Stamp Tool in Photoshop

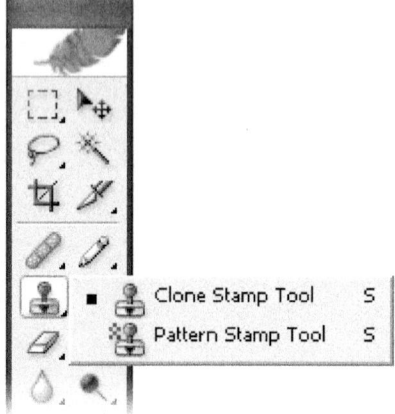

The clone stamp tool in Photoshop enables you to replicate a portion of a picture.

Setting a sample point in the picture that will be used as a reference to generate a fresh cloned region is the first step in the process.

- Choose the Clone Stamp tool from the drop-down menu. Check the settings in the options menu for the Clone Stamp tool. Make sure you have the right brush size for the task. The following are some common settings:

1. If you choose this option, the new cloned picture will be drawn constantly, even if you let go of the mouse button while drawing. If this option is unchecked, the clone will start drawing from the sampling point each time you leave the mouse and return to painting.
2. **Use All Layers:** If this option is chosen, data from all visible layers will be used. Otherwise, the active layer will be the only one utilized.

Photoshop Paint Bucket Tool

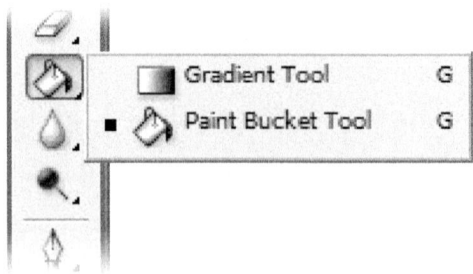

Based on color similarity, the paint bucket tool fills a portion of a picture. The paint bucket will fill an area surrounding the pixel you selected when you click anywhere in the picture.

The size of the filled area is determined by how similar each adjacent pixel is to the one you clicked on. The tolerance value may be changed in the options toolbar to modify this parameter (make sure the paint bucket tool is selected first). A low tolerance affects only colors that are extremely close; a large tolerance affects more pixels. The range is 0 (precise color matching only) to 255 (all other color combinations) (all colors).

In the options bar, you may also change the following things:

- **Fill:** Pattern or Foreground color (currently chosen color). When you choose pattern, the next drop-menu appears, allowing you to select a pattern.
- Normal, dissolve, brighten, darken, and other "blending modes" are available, as are many additional tools.
- Reduce the opacity to partly reveal the underlying picture.
- **Anti-alias:** Makes edges smoother by mixing adjacent pixels progressively.

Contiguous:

When working with several layers, the fill is created by combining all of them (otherwise only the selected layer is used).

Fill in the Blanks

Only pixels that are linked to the original pixel are filled when the contiguous checkbox is checked. This is shown by the example below. The picture is clicked at the left edge, first with contiguous on, then off:

Adobe Photoshop for Beginners

Additional Info:
- Locking the layer's transparency Layers palette prevents transparent regions from being filled.
- In bitmap mode, the paint bucket tool won't work.

Magic Wand Tool

The Magic Wand tool is layered alongside the Quick Selection tool in the Tools panels, fourth from the top. Simply click and hold on a certain tool to view the additional tools available in that place to access a stacked tool. The tiny black triangle in the bottom right hand corner of the symbol indicates stacked tools.

The Magic Wand tool's Options bar features are crucial to its functioning.

- **Tolerance:** This setting controls how much of the picture is chosen when you click on a certain area.
- A number of 10 indicates that depending on the location where you clicked, 5 darker and 5 lighter values will be selected.
- **Anti-alias:** Improves the smoothness of selection edges.
- **Contiguous:** Only pixels in the same row are chosen when this option is selected. When this box is unchecked, all pixels within the specified Tolerance value are selected.
- **Sample All Layers:** If selected, will examine all layers rather than just the highlighted one.

Other icons in the Magic Wands Options panel enable us to make more precise choices.

- Make a fresh pick.
- A new selection to an old one
- Subtract from a previously chosen option.
- Choose the point where two choices meet.

TWO

How to Open Files

Open Files

The File menu, like with other applications, has the option to open a file. Ctrl-O/Cmd-O (PC/Mac) is a keyboard shortcut for this operation.

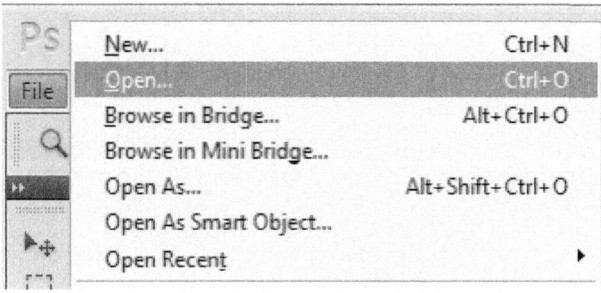

Adobe Photoshop for Beginners

The Open dialogue box will display once you've chosen to open a file. You may access your files and pictures from here.

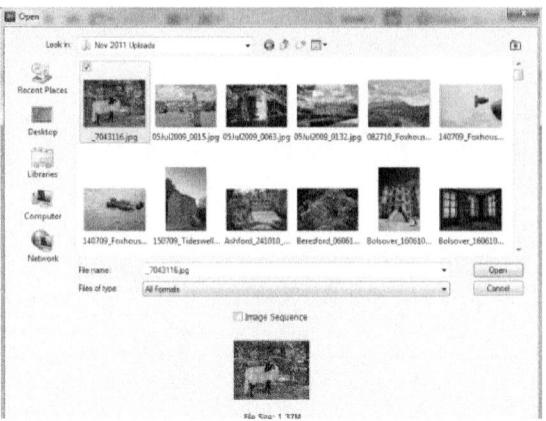

Open As

There is now an option to Open As in the File menu, in addition to the usual Open option. The Open As dialogue box is nearly identical to the Open dialogue box, with the exception that it allows you to open an image in one format and have it appear in Photoshop in another format.

How to Open Files

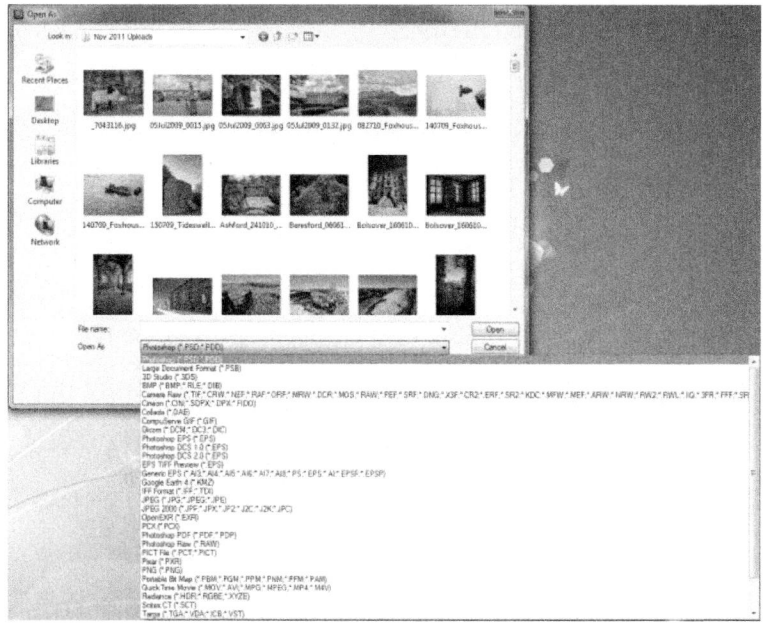

The Open As command can open most single-layered file types as Camera Raw documents, which is a handy feature. This will launch the Camera Raw plugin, which is included with Adobe Photoshop. You can quickly and easily make simple adjustments to your image without having to learn complicated Photoshop editing techniques.

Open As Smart Object

Open As Smart Object is the third option. A Smart Object allows you to make non-destructive edits to your image and is particularly useful if you plan to make extensive edits or multiple transformations, such as scaling. Smart objects have a small icon in the bottom right corner of the Layers panel, and if you apply a filter to them, the filter will appear below the layer.

The application of a filter to a Smart Object is temporary, and you can change the settings at any time by double-clicking on the filter name in the Layers panel.

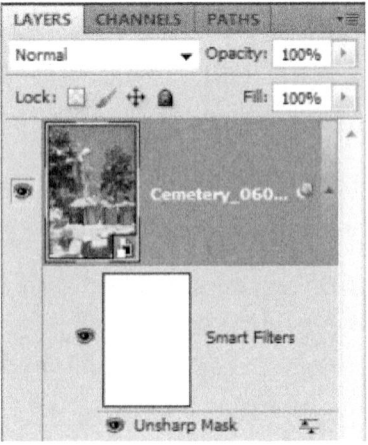

Aside from dragging an image onto the work area, there are a few other ways to get an image into Photoshop. You may now choose between Bridge and Mini-Bridge for file browsing.

How to Save Your Work

It's critical to save your completed design after finishing a design or making an image edit in Adobe Photoshop so that you don't lose it. You can save your design and open it later, as well as share it with family and friends.

The drawbacks of not saving your design on Adobe are that you will have to start over or start a new project.

Here are a few things to familiarize yourself with when it comes to saving your design on Adobe:

1. To save your design after you've finished working on it, go to File, then Save, then **"Save As,"** and give it a name you'll remember (**NB: Try as much as possible to save your new work with a name you can remember easily, so you won't be confused when looking for the job you are handling**).

Adobe Photoshop for Beginners

2. It's also worth noting that saving your work in Photoshop format (.psd) preserves the same type, layers, and additional editable Photoshop thins. Experts advise that you save your PSD format design, especially when working on it.
3. Users can also save their images or designs in PNG (.png) and JPEG (.jpg) formats. It will save as a standard photo file if you do it this way, allowing you to share it.

How to Open Files

4. It will also be possible to launch it from other applications and even make it available on the internet. You can save a design in either PNG or JPEG format once you've completed the image editing procedures.

Saving an image relieves the stress of having to start over, especially if you forget the steps you took to edit the image. Rather than regretting it later, it is recommended that you save images as time passes in case your computer or device crashes.

Save your work in the following methods:

PSD: This is Photoshop's native file format, and it's the one that will offer you the greatest freedom if you exclusively use Photoshop for picture editing. It will save all of the layers, changes, and effects you've used on your picture. This format can also handle files with a high bit depth of up to 32 bits. Because the file sizes for high bit depth files may be enormous, think twice before storing your picture in anything other than 8 bits.

TIFF: The Tagged-Image File Format (TIFF, TIF) has many of the same characteristics as PSD (when opened in Photoshop). This format is important since it is compatible with nearly all image-opening applications. It also enables you to decrease the size of your file by using a variety of compression techniques.

JPEG: The Joint Photographic Experts Group (JPEG, JPG) format is mostly used for pictures that will be seen on a computer screen or on the internet. This file format employs "Lossy" compression, which means that data is lost during the compression process, resulting in a smaller file but at the expense of picture quality. If your camera only captures JPEG pictures, I suggest saving the image as a PSD while editing since continuously opening and saving JPEG files causes recompression and may significantly damage the data.

GIF: Graphics Interchange Format (GIF) is a file format for displaying graphics in indexed color mode. Because this file format can only hold 256 colors, it is seldom used for photos. It does, however, have a number of features that have helped it become extremely popular in online graphics. • Small file size •

Allows for transparency • Allows for animation

PNG: Similar to GIF, this format is used for online graphics. The PNG format is far more versatile than the GIF format in terms of supporting 24bit photographic pictures and various color modes. However, web browsers do not support it as extensively. When we discuss storing pictures for the web in book three of this series, we'll go over the JPEG, GIF, and PNG formats in more depth.

PDF: The Portable Document Format (PDF) is a file format that can be seen on a variety of systems and apps. It supports compression, 16-bit format, and standard color modes while preserving text, vector, and raster information, as well as Photoshop editing (if selected).

What Is the Best Way to Undo a Command?

You may quickly undo one or more actions in Adobe Photoshop's History section. Undoing a command simply means returning to your original state before it was cleaned or deleted.

If you are working on a picture in Adobe and accidentally erase or delete it, you may always reverse a command and restore the prior functioning image before deleting it.

To reverse the previous operation you were working on, follow the instructions below:

1. To begin, open Adobe Photoshop.
2. Select edit from the drop-down menu.
3. Finally, choose **Undo** (Mac users should use Command + Z, while Windows users should pick Control + Z).

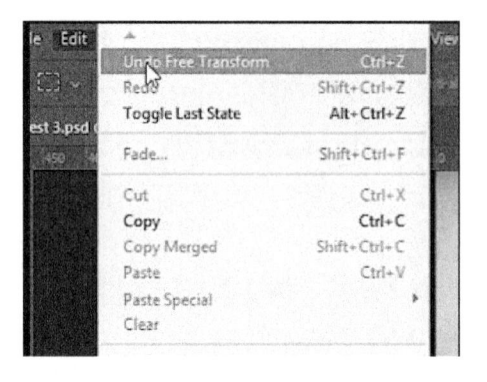

4. When you're finished, your prior item or operation will be restored, and you'll be able to work on it again.

How to Open Files

You can quickly recover the many operations or items you were previously working on if you were working on several things at the same time (not just one).

To reverse the many procedures or items you were previously working on, follow the instructions below:

1. To begin, open **Adobe Photoshop**.
2. Select edit from the drop-down menu.
3. Then search for the option that says **"Step backward many times" and choose it (NB: If you don't want to go through the given options, you may attempt another choice. You must select a technique or action in the History section if you choose the alternate option)**. The History section's selected option must tally or perform the function of undoing all of the tasks you were doing on Adobe.

Finally, Adobe Photoshop 2021 includes a feature that allows users to undo the previous task they were working on. Working on a task or operation again is simply referred to as redoing it.

To learn how to redo a task in Adobe Photoshop, follow the steps below:

Adobe Photoshop for Beginners

1. Open Adobe.
2. Find and select the Edit option.
3. Locate and select Redo. (NB: On second thought, if you want to redo a task on a Mac or Windows computer, you have other options. For example, Mac users can redo a task or operation by pressing Command + Z on their keyboard, whereas Windows users can redo a task or operation by pressing Control + Z on their keyboard).

THREE

Spot Healing Tool

This application allows you to fix picture flaws such as blemishes, pimples, scratches, and more. It operates by scanning the working area or following a predetermined path and introducing the mistakes into other areas of the picture.

This Adobe device may be found in the toolbox list on the left side of your device screen.

1. **Create a new blank layer.**

- In the Layers panel of the newly opened photo in Photoshop, we can see that we only have one layer, the Background layer, which contains our image:
- In Photoshop, the Layers panel shows the original image on the Background layer.
- Even though we want to improve the photo, we also want to protect the original, so we'll add a new blank layer above the Background layer. On this separate layer, we'll do all of our spot healing. At the bottom of the Layers panel, click the New Layer icon:

2. Change the name of the new layer

Photoshop creates a new blank layer above the Background layer, but it is named Layer 1 by default. That doesn't tell us much about what the layer is for, so in the Layers panel, double-click on the layer's name and rename it "spot healing." When retouching images, it's common to end up with a lot of layers, so giving each one a descriptive name makes it easier to keep track of them. When you're finished, press Enter (Windows) or Return (Mac) to accept the new name: Renaming the new layer.

3. **Choose a Spot Healing Brush.**

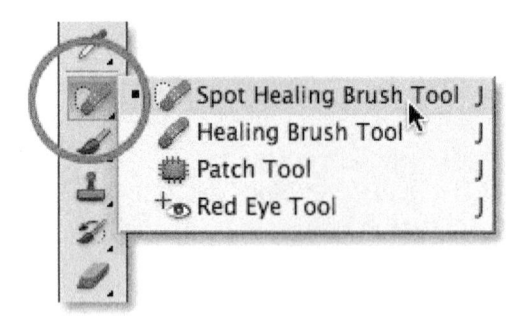

From the Tools panel, choose the Spot Healing Brush. It's in the same section as the other healing tools. If the Spot Healing Brush is not visible, click on it and keep your mouse button down for a second or two until a little fly-out menu appears, then pick the Spot Healing Brush from the menu. The Spot Healing Brush is kept in the same category as the other healing tools.

4. **Select "Sample All Layers" from the drop-down menu.**

The Spot Healing Brush only works with the layer that is presently chosen in the Layers window by default. If we attempt to utilize it right now, we'll run

Spot Healing Tool

into some issues since we have a blank layer selected, which means we'll only be able to replace nothing with different nothing. We must also instruct Photoshop to examine the picture on the Background layer. To do so, go to the Options Bar at the top of the screen and choose Sample All Layers:

5. **Select "Content-Aware" from the drop-down menu.**

Type: ○ Proximity Match ○ Create Texture ● Content-Aware ☑ Sample All Layers

Make sure Content-Aware is selected in the Options Bar if you're using Photoshop CS5 or later. This is a new feature in CS5 that enables the Spot Healing Brush to find a better substitute texture for the issue region you've clicked on by leveraging texture from the surrounding area. You won't be able to use Content-Aware if you're running CS4 or earlier. In such situation, you should use Proximity Match, which may still provide excellent results:

For the greatest results, choose Content-Aware (or Proximity Match for CS4 and earlier users).

6. **To Heal the Problem Spots, Click On Them.**

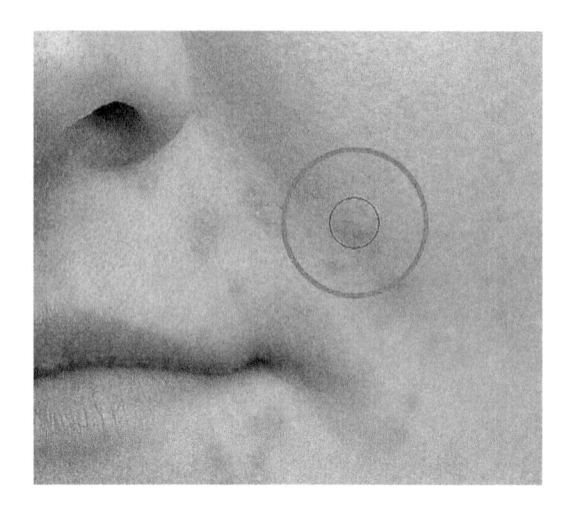

- All we have to do now is click on problem places in the picture to correct them using the Spot Healing Brush, Sample All Layers, and Content-Aware (or Proximity Match).
- Make the brush cursor a little bigger than the issue region by using the keyboard shortcut.
- Use the Spot Healing Brush to click on the pimple, and it'll vanish, replaced with excellent texture from the surrounding area.

Spot Healing Tool

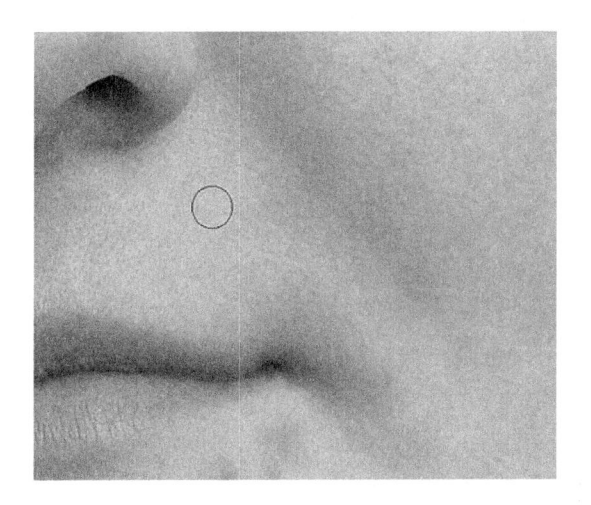

As previously said, the Spot Healing Brush sometimes make mistakes, so if this occurs, just hit Ctrl+Z (Windows) / Command+Z (Mac) to undo the error and try again. You'll receive a different outcome each time you attempt.

How to Use the Brush Tool

You may use the brush tool to draw or sketch a picture. It works by left-clicking and moving your cursor over the picture you want to draw.

Additionally, the brush paints with straight edges, and the following choices are available underneath it:

- Mode
- Flow
- Brush
- Opacity

Erasing Tool

To discover this specific tool, go through the second set of icons in the toolbox. Additionally, the eraser tool is divided into three types: magic eraser, eraser, and background eraser. Overall, this tool is a brush that clears or eliminates pixels as they travel over a picture. When you choose the eraser tool, you have the following options:

- Opacity
- Airbrush
- Mode
- Erase to history
- Brush
- Flow

Magic Wand Tool

This Adobe tool allows you to choose a portion of a picture based on its color type. This tool may also be found at the top side of the toolbox.

Using a magic wand to choose a portion of a picture will change the color of the whole image. You may choose the various choices to know the exact Selection you have, just as you do with other tools.

Check out the steps below to learn how to utilize this tool:

Adobe Photoshop for Beginners

- Select the magic wand tool from the tool list.

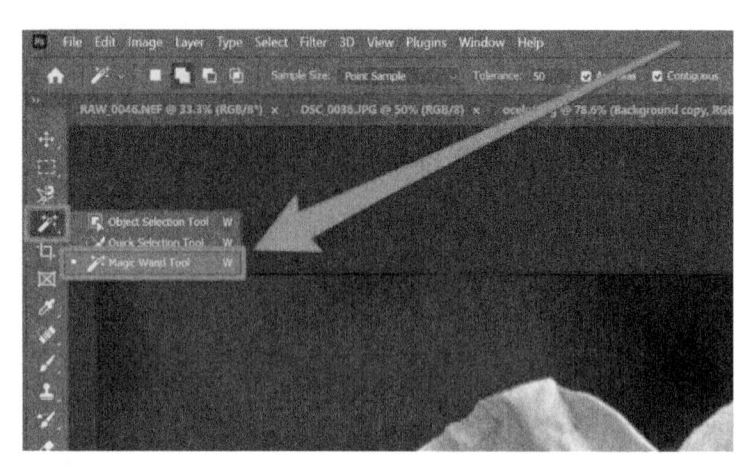

- Select a Tolerance value from the options menu. The amount of tolerance values indicates how well colors match. **Note: A higher tolerance value will equate to a bigger selection.**

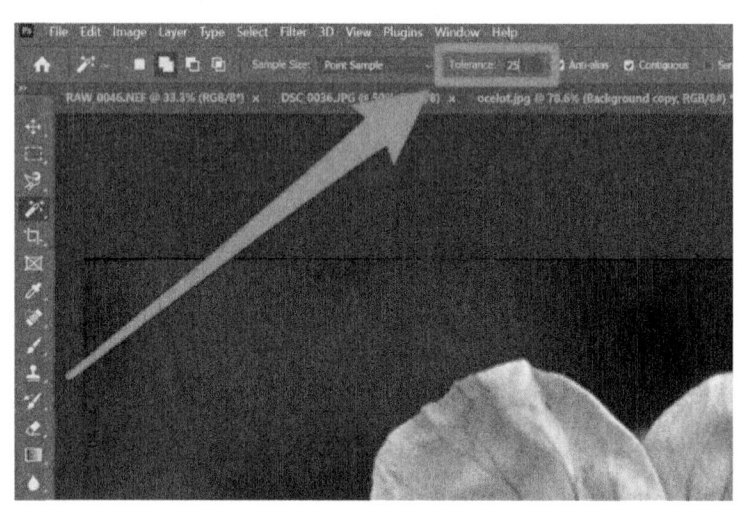

Spot Healing Tool

- Select regions from all layers by selecting View All Layers.
- Use anti-aliased viewing to position a smooth corner of your choosing.
- Select the connected regions by seeing contiguous.
- In the place where you want to checkmark, choose the picture. (**Note: By using the Shift and Alt buttons, you may add and delete items from the Selection.** This may also be done by going to the settings menu and choosing the selection keys).

How to Work With Layers and the Magic Wand Tool

Using layers to ensure that you don't inadvertently alter portion of the image that you want to save is a fantastic method to ensure that you don't make any mistakes. If you're planning to use the Magic Wand tool to perform a large change, duplicate your layers first.

This maintains the image's original state and allows you to combine the two versions if desired. To do so, follow these steps:

1. Open the Layers palette on the right side of the screen and drag the current layer(s) to the **"Create a New Layer"** button at the bottom of the screen (formed like a plus sign or sticky note).
2. Click the eye symbol next to your original layers to hide them. Drag the layer to the bottom of the window's New Layer button.

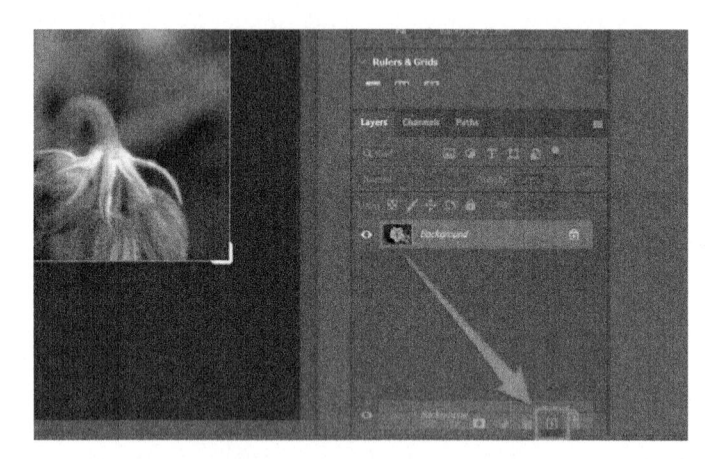

3. Select the new layers by clicking on them and then selecting and modifying them. Make sure the layer you're not working with is hidden.

Spot Healing Tool

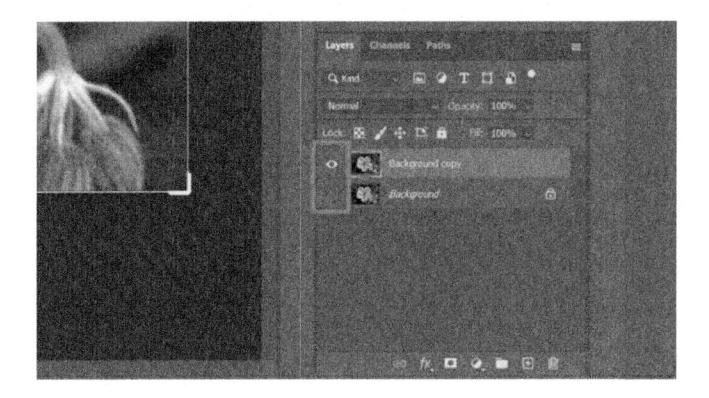

You may utilize the eye icons to conceal and unhide the layers as needed, which is useful if you wish to reference the originals.

FOUR

Adobe Photoshop Toolbox

The Adobe toolbox contains the most common tools for editing or doing other tasks on a photograph. To utilize any Adobe product, all you have to do is choose one and start using it. Any tool in the Adobe toolbox has a little arrow next to it. As a result, this tool shows that it has more choices available. Select any tool in Adobe and hold down the left mouse button to see its capabilities and other functions.

Select and hold the select tool, for example, to display several choices, such as single row selection or other selection options.

Cropping Tool

This tool is also included in Adobe Photoshop, and it allows you to choose a portion of a picture and ignore anything else outside of the photo area. The crop tool is located on the third side of the toolbox, towards the top. Even if the cropping tool reduces the height and breadth of a picture, it is not considered resizing. Images may be enlarged via resizing, while cropping simply lowers them.

Examine the following methods for using the crop tool:

1. Select and open the crop tool from the toolbox and list of available tools.
2. Select a portion of a picture to keep. **Note: This is very similar to creating a normal selection.**
3. The portion to be held will be highlighted after you remove your fingers from the mouse.
4. After that, you may choose to modify the crop area by sliding the handles of your choosing.
5. To complete the cropping procedure, place your hands on the Enter button.
6. After that, your chosen picture will be cropped and shrunk according to your preferences (**NB:**

Users should know that they can attach and use resizing and cropping tools in the same image they are working on).

Clone Stamp Tool

This tool allows you to double-click on a portion of a picture. Furthermore, the methods need the placement of a sample point in the image that will serve as a reference for cloning a new one.

Simply choose the clone stamp tool from the tool list, review the settings in the options sections, and double-check that the brush size is correct.

The clone stamp tool has a number of extra features, including:

- **Using All Layers:** Selecting this option implies that all visible layers will have an impact on your data.

- **Aligned:** If you choose this option, the freshly cloned picture will be drawn without a number of times even after you remove your hands from your screen or mouse. To stop the ongoing activity, just untick the option.

Lightroom vs. Photoshop

Photoshop and Lightroom are two digital photography editing apps with a variety of features designed to meet the needs of users. While Photoshop is essential in every photographer's life, Lightroom outperforms it when it comes to managing and operating thousands of pictures on your device.

Furthermore, Photoshop's foundation is based on modifying images to make them appear free of flaws. So, when should we employ Photoshop or Lightroom?

When Should I Use Lightroom?

Lightroom is primarily intended for professional photographers to use and run. It works well for organizing photos and making minor adjustments to them.

You may choose between Adobe Photoshop Lightroom Classic and Lightroom in Lightroom. The former is a desktop application that allows you to save pictures locally, such as on your hard disk. Lightroom, on the other hand, allows you to save files to the cloud.

Adobe Photoshop Toolbox

What Can You Do Using Lightroom?

- **Editing:** Simply enter the Develop Module once you've imported your files to enhance and alter the pictures. You may modify them in this option to improve your image from all angles. To make your pictures look beautiful and appealing, just enhance the color and light, sharpen, and add additional effects. Additionally, when utilizing Lightroom to its maximum potential, presets save time. Through the discovery interactive edit feature, users may create their own presets or select to download several presets. To reduce red-eye effects, remove spots with a healing brush, and make your teeth look white, you don't need to launch Photoshop. Additionally, Lightroom allows users to make changes to a picture without altering the original image.

- **Organization:** Another instance why Lightroom comes in handy is when you're organizing your files. Lightroom is used by many photographers to begin the editing process since it excels at handling a large number of photos at once. Lightroom makes it simple to manage, organize, arrange, and find pictures in a certain area. You can also assign ratings to pictures to help you choose the finest photos for your collections and albums.

Photoshop

Now that we've covered the occasions when Lightroom is required, let's flip around and see when Photoshop may be utilized. Photoshop is essential when it comes to controlling, creating, and improving photographs. It's the ideal option for pictures that need pixel-level detail. Fine painters and image retouchers may start using Lightroom, but because of the incredible capabilities it offers, they will quickly switch to Photoshop.

Photoshop may be used for the following tasks:

- **Layers:** By investigating smart things, objects, and even layers in Photoshop, you may work or function in a non-destructive manner. Layer masking may be used to enhance a picture created using layers. You may also alter and touch again as a result of this. On your picture, you can also obtain a layer for white balance or color adjustments, a layer with a blue sky, a layer with a drab sky, and so on. Layers have a learning curve and are ideal for improving images after they've been produced.

- **Retouch:** Photoshop has a variety of editing tools that may alter the content and appearance of a picture. Unlike Lightroom, which focuses on minor adjustments and editing, Photoshop is ideal for making significant changes to a picture. Using content-aware technologies in Photoshop, you may remove perplexing elements or objects. Alternatively, you may combine multiple photos to create a composite, or you can use several images to create photo-realistic visuals. When it comes to combining several images, graphic designers are not left out. They can accomplish this using vector graphics and text. The foundations of Photoshop include masking, layers, Photoshop effects, and change controls, which significantly enable users to modify and alter pictures.

- **Wrapping Up:** Knowing the differences between Photoshop and Lightroom can help you choose the best photo editor for a certain design job. It makes no difference whatever kind you select. Both of them are designed to function well together. Users may work on a picture in Lightroom and then choose E to transfer it to Photoshop for additional editing.

What Is a RAW File?

The picture files must be delivered into camera RAW before any modification can be done. Photoshop may be used to open these files.

To access RAW files in the file browser, follow the steps below:

- Double-click or touch the File icon twice.
- Alternatively, you may open with Adobe by clicking the right-hand side on Windows or holding Ctrl and clicking on a Mac.

Creating a Collaborative Album and Asking Others to Participate

Users may create a group album and invite others to see it or contribute to it. You may also select pictures that aren't in the album and send them out as an invite with a request for contributions. You may also get access to all of your favorite pictures using this technique.

Go through the following steps to create a shared album and invite people:

1. Begin by making a new album. **Note: Alternatively, you can choose a previous album from the Albums list.** You may also choose several pictures from the Grid list. After you've made your decision, you may choose from the following options:

    - On your device's screen, tap the Share and Invite symbol in the upper right corner of the grid list.
    - Select the Share and Invite option.

2. Select the option to Enable Sharing from the Share and Invite area.

3. The Link Access section is set to Invite Only by default. This option creates a private link that only the people you invite may view and contribute to. Meanwhile, you may change the choice so that others can see and contribute as well.
4. Copy the URL and share it with others. If the Link Access is set to Anyone may see, you can simply share the album by clicking the Twitter or Facebook buttons. Simply enter their email address in the invite box and choose Invite if you want to manually invite others to contribute or see your album. After that, the individuals you invited will get an email with instructions on how to access your album.
5. In the Invite box, you'll see a list of the email addresses to whom you've sent invitations. A drop-down option next to the email addresses organizes an individual's album access settings. From there, you may do the following tasks:

- Contribute: Allow your guests to add photos to the shared album, mark them as favorites, and leave comments on the photos that have been uploaded.

Adobe Photoshop Toolbox

- Remove: Delete or remove a specific invitee from the list.
- View: Allows others to view the shared album as well as a lot more.

6. While you're still in the Share and Invite box, click the Customize label to view and change the following settings:

    - Theme: Decide how you'd want to organize the pictures you'd like to share. You may choose from a variety of themes, including column, one-up, and picture grid.
    - Album title: Display the title of the album. You may also untick any of these to make the name disappear or take longer to appear. The preceding album name is shown by default. Meanwhile, presuming you've selected a set of pictures in the grid, the time and date the link was created will be shown as Title.
    - Appearance: To determine the color tone of the pictures, choose between bright and dark.

Adobe Photoshop for Beginners

- Author: Display the name of the person who generated the link. Remove the check mark from the option to delay or conceal the name. Users may also choose Customize on the web to change the order of pictures in the shared album.

7. Go to the Settings area and make any of the following changes:

    - Allow likes and comments: This option is enabled by default, allowing your visitors to leave comments and likes on your shared photos. You may either keep it ticked or untick it to disallow viewers to like and comment, depending on your preference.
    - Allow JPG downloads: Check or uncheck this box to allow others to download the shared picture group.
    - Reveal location data: Tick this box to allow others to view the location information in shared group photos, or untick it to conceal location data.

- Allow people to view metadata of group pictures: Select this option to allow others to access information of group photos.
- Allow access requests: You may allow others to seek access to shared photos here.

When the whole procedure is finished, choose Done (**NB: Now, your group album is formed, and you can make others contribute as invitees**).

To accept an invitation, follow the procedures below:

- Open the email invitation sent by the album owner and choose View album from the drop-down menu.
- In the Lightroom desktop program, go to the left-hand side and touch the people symbol.
- Choose Shared with You to view a list of group albums that have been given to you. Select your chosen album to see it from there.
- If the owner of the group album gives you permission to participate, you have the option to do the following: Use the grid view to add pictures, Use the add icon to add pictures, select

images from Albums and My Photos to add to your collage.
- Select Add Photo from the Add Photo box to add star ratings, GPS locations, and keywords.
- When you're finished, press the **Add Photo key.**

FIVE

How Can I Export My Photos?

PNG, Original, JPEG, and TIF are all options for exporting changed pictures.

Follow the steps below to complete this procedure:

1. Open the picture in Loupe display that you want to export.
2. Next, go to the Grid display and press and hold the picture you want to pick to access the multi-selection display. Mark all of the pictures you want to export with a checkmark.
3. Then, on the upper right-hand side of your device's screen, choose the share icon.

4. Select the Export as an option from the menu that appears.
5. Select one of the following choices from the Export menu:

- Choose from PNG, JPG, Original, and TIF as your file type.
- Preset: To quickly export your photos as JPG and Original, go to the preset area.
- Watermark: After exporting pictures, you may add a watermark text here.
- Quality: Choose from a range of 10% to 100%.
- Dimensions: TIF and JPG files may have dimensions added to them. The dimension choices are shown below:
  - Small: The length of the saved TIF and JPG pictures is reduced to 2048 pixels. In addition, the width is calculated based on the initial aspect ratio.
  - Custom: This affects the biggest image corner's selected pixel value and works with the picture's initial aspect ratio to

How Can I Export My Photos?

    measure the second corner.

   o The largest available dimensions are as follows: Both TIF and JPG formats are available for exporting the selected pictures in the greatest available dimension.

6. Using the extra choices, you will be able to get access to:

- Naming the files
- Metadata
- Ample color space
- Caption
- Information about the location
- RAW data from the camera

7. Finally, choose the quantity of pictures you want to export and finish the procedure.

Filters

Filters are unique effects used to enhance the beauty and attractiveness of photographs. Users of Adobe Photoshop may apply various filter effects depending on their preferences.

How can I browse through the filter gallery?

The variety of filters included with Photoshop is one of the numerous features that sets it apart from other picture editors. A variety of third-party filters are available in addition to the enormous number of built-in filters. Filters may adjust the colors of a picture as well as increase the image's quality. The Filter Gallery was created to make it simpler to view how filters will appear on your picture once they've been applied, as well as to discover the filter you're searching for.

Filters are ideal for bringing out the finest in a picture or enhancing the attractiveness of a photograph. By opening the Filter Gallery in Photoshop, you may add or apply stunning filters.

Follow the steps below to go through the filter gallery and add filters:

- Select the item, object, or picture you wish to change from a layer.
- Before opening the Filter Gallery, go to the menu section and choose Filters.
- From here, you may experiment with and test various filters, changing their parameters to get your desired result.

- Add additional filters to the Filter Gallery and change their stacking list to investigate or test more items and more parts.
- Click OK to close or close the Filter Gallery and keep the filters you specified before. **Note: Users are also allowed to apply filters after you have formed a selection to apply filters to only a particular spot you have chosen.**

How to Use Smart Filters to Blur a Picture

A Photoshop smart filter that can be modified may be used to blur images. The only thing you're allowed to do is apply or put the blue filter.

To finish this procedure, follow the steps below:

- Select a layer that you are comfortable with, as well as a layer that contains the object or items you want to obscure. **(Note: A layer could be a background or anything at all).**
- Select the Filter option.
- Select the option to convert for smart filters and then touch OK to complete the process. **Note: Once done with this option, the chosen or marked layer will be converted into a layer that will allow for modifying filters.**

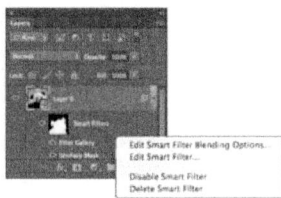

- Select filter once more while you still have a similar layer selected.
- Next, go to Blur and then to the "Gaussian Blur" option.
- Change the Radius control in the top blur area until you get the amount of Blur shown in the live preview.
- Select OK if you wish to apply the Gaussian Blue filter here.
- Keep in mind that in the Layers area, the Smart Filter is linked to your picture layer. **Note: This option permits you to change the filter settings easily.**
- To finish the procedure, just click twice on the Gaussian Blur Smart Filter in the Layers section

and make a change in the Gaussian Blur section that appears before choosing OK.

Finally, save the picture in Photoshop format with the modifications you've made. **Note: Saving the changed image will hold the smart filter layer.**

SIX

How to Use a Layer Mask to Substitute a Background Picture

A layer mask may be used to completely cover over a single backdrop with another picture.

Consider the following options for completing this task:

1. Start with two layers. The first picture should be placed on the top layer, while the bottom layer should include another background image.
2. Go to the Layers section and double-check that the top layer is selected or marked.
3. Go to the Tools area and choose the Quick Selection tool to use.

4. Select the parts of the first picture that you do not wish to delete in their entirety.
5. Select the **"Add layer mask"** option under the Layers section and add a layer mask thumbnail to the top layer. **Note: The layer mask will conceal everything except what you've highlighted. Additionally, the higher layer's concealed portions will allow you to see down through the layer stack to the bottom layer's auxiliary backdrop.**

How to Use a Layer Mask to Add an Item to a Picture

You may also use a layer mask to add or remove an object or item from a picture. Follow the steps below to use a layer mask to add an object to a photo:

How to Use a Layer Mask to Substitute a Background Picture

1. Start with a double layer. The picture containing the object or item you wish to add should be on the top layer, with the initial photo on the bottom layer.
2. Go to the Layers section and choose or mark the top layer.
3. Go to the bottom Layers area and choose "Add layer mask" from the drop-down menu. (**Note that the choice includes a white thumbnail or rectangle that is linked to the top layer.**)
4. The layer mask is sometimes regarded to be the white layer. The layer mask also determines which side of the connecting layer is visible and which is not. Furthermore, the white color on the mask denotes the portions that are visible, while the black color denotes the parts that are not visible.
5. Select or click the Brush tool from the Tools menu. Simply paint with white or black colors to make the sections of the linked layer visible or not after you've checked or selected the mask thumbnail in the Layers section.

What Is the Best Way to Make a Graphic Shape in Adobe Photoshop?

Aside from words, pictures may also have shapes added to them to beautify them and make them more appealing to look at. When you have the proper knowledge, applying shapes to pictures is a simple procedure.

Examine the following methods for incorporating shapes into images:

1. To view all of the shape tools, open the tools panel and pick and push firmly on the Rectangle tool. You may then choose the form tool you want to use and the one you want to draw with.
2. Select a Fill color and other shape lists from the options area (**Note: Be aware that the selected options in this part can be changed at another time**).

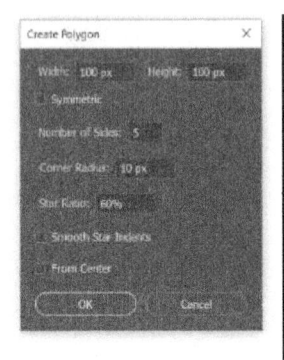

How to Use a Layer Mask to Substitute a Background Picture

3. While dragging the shape in a picture to create an editable shape, press firmly on the Shift button to avoid modifications to the shape (**Note: Doing this will automatically create a new shape layer**).
4. Move the shape to the correct location in the picture using the Move tool (**Note: Take your time here since you don't want to make any errors that may impact the final image result**).
5. Use Edit and Free Transform to turn, alter, or scale a shape without compromising its quality. Mac users should pick Command + T, while Windows users should select Control + T.
6. If you want to change the color of a form, go to the layers menu and look for the shape layer you want to change. To open the Color Picker, double-tap the thumbnail on the layer after you've seen or found it.
7. While selecting the colors in the color picker, you will also find a live preview of the chosen colors in shape. In addition, after you've found the color you desire, choose OK to see the modifications.

What is the Best Way to Add Texture to a Photograph?

Using Photoshop's blend modes, you can create a textured design.

To finish this procedure, follow the steps below:

1. Begin by making double layers. Be aware that the photo with the texture you want to include should reside on the upper layer, and the main photo should be placed on the lower layer.
2. Go to the Layers tab and make sure the top layer is selected or marked.
3. Change the blend mode in the menu that appears in the top left-hand corner of the layer section. It should be set to Overlay. **Note: Normally, it is set to Normal.**

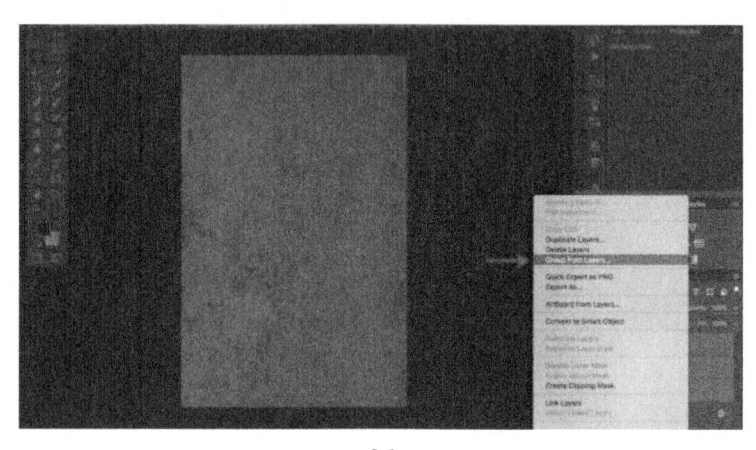

How to Use a Layer Mask to Substitute a Background Picture

4. Once you've finished the preceding steps, the color texture will change and the colors of the bottom layer will be affected. In this stage, you may experiment with a few different blend modes to discover which one works best with your pictures.

5. Go to the top Layers area and tweak or experiment with the Opacity slider to change or alter the texture of the picture.

SEVEN

How to Create a Custom Shape That Is Already Built-in in Adobe Photoshop

You are not just limited to using standard forms in your pictures, but you are also permitted to utilize bespoke shapes.

Look at the steps below to see how to complete this step:

1. Go to the Tools menu, then pick the Rectangle tool and push down firmly. It is important to note that in most instances, you may not find the rectangle tool, so you have to select any other tool you can see).

2. Go ahead and choose the **Custom Shape tool** from there.
3. Go to the settings section and choose the lower pointer on the right-hand side of the Shape picker.
4. Select the gear icon on the Shape picker's right-hand side if you want to view all of the custom shapes you can apply to pictures. Then, on the following page, choose OK after selecting the "All" option. Similarly, choose the bottom right border of the Form Picker and drag it to see the whole shape.

Text

Create visible messages on a picture and share them with your friends and family at any time.

How to Insert/Add Text

You may be required to put text in a photograph as part of a design assignment. It's a straightforward design that just needs a basic understanding of the processes.

Examine the following methods for adding text to a photograph:

How to Create a Custom Shape That Is Already Built-in . . .

1. Select the Horizontal Type tool from the tools panel.

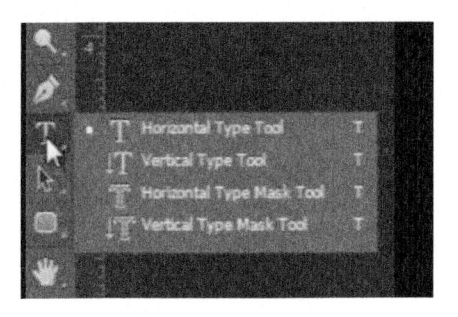

2. Select font size, color, font, and other choices that will give value to your content under the options area. **Note: In this option, you are allowed to modify the listed settings.**
3. Choose the canvas and type one line of text. You may also create a text paragraph by moving out of a text box and putting text into the box.
4. To agree to the content, choose the checkbox in the choices area, and then exit the text mode. **Note: Performing this act means that it will automatically form a new layer that can be modified anytime you like.**

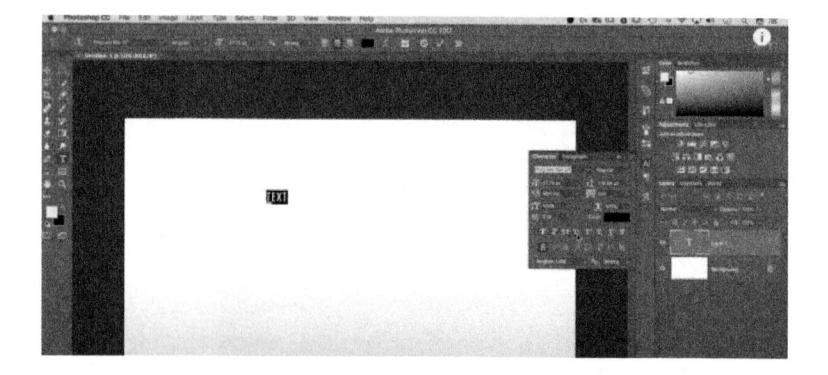

5. Continue the procedure by dragging your text to the desired location in your picture using the Move tool.
6. When you're finished, save your finished text picture. If you don't save your finished picture, all of your edits and alterations will be lost.

Note: Saving completed text images should be carried out in the Photoshop format.

How to Edit Text

You've completed a text picture, but you're not happy with what you've written? You can always go back and make changes to a text that was previously typed in an image. When you edit a text in a picture, you're essentially replacing what was previously written with a whole new text.

How to Create a Custom Shape That Is Already Built-in . . .

Consider the following options for completing this task:

1. Let's say you want to change the wording on a layer type. In such scenario, choose the layer type in the layers section and then the Vertical or Horizontal Type tool in the tools section. **Note: Make any necessary changes or adjustments to the options section settings. The color of the text, for example, or the font size are some of the options that may be changed.**

2. To finish your saving, click the checkbox in the choices area once you've finished altering or changing the already written text in the picture to another.

EIGHT

Color

Adobe Photoshop's color palette is extremely important. It reveals a lot about how you look, how an image appears, and how image intensity is presented.

What are the best ways to utilize background and foreground colors?

Save Colors in both the background and foreground color areas in Adobe:

Here are some things to keep in mind when it comes to background and foreground colors:

- The type tool, the shape tool, the brush tool, and other color-related operations may be found in

the bottom left-hand corner of the tools section in the floor foreground region.
- You may set or change the foreground color in a variety of ways. Users may, for example, choose the eyedropper tool. Users may alternatively utilize the swatches panel, color panel, or color picker as an alternative.
- To quickly switch between background and foreground regions, choose the two-pointed arrow on the top of the two-color spaces or press and hold the **X button**.
- The background color area is located below the foreground color area and allows you to save a completely different color.

What Is the Best Way to Choose a Color?

You may choose various colors using the swatches option, color panel, and color picker.

Take a look at the following examples of how to utilize the various color options:

Option of using swatches:

If the swatches option does not appear on your screen, go to the menu option and choose **Windows** before clicking on Swatches.

1. To utilize the swatches option, choose a swatch, a colored square in the swatches option, to change the foreground color to the swatch color of your choice.

Using the color palette:

If you happen to miss the color panel on your device's screen, just go to the menu option and choose Window before selecting Color.

1. The color panel functions in the same way as the small color picker. Users may choose a color hue from the slider and adjust the saturation and brightness to suit their preference for contrast. Furthermore, the color you choose will appear in the foreground color box in the tools section.
2. In addition, compared to the color picker, the color panel does not offer nearly as many choices. However, utilizing the color panel has the advantage of allowing it to stay open on your screen for quick input.

How to Use a Color Picker:

- To open the color picker, first choose the foreground color box under the tools panel. There are many approaches you may take to do this:
- The first option allows you to enter exact color values in the RGB, Hexadecimal, HSB, and CMYK color spaces.
- The second method is to simply adjust the vertical slider while the color picker is open to choose a color. You'll also be asked to choose a location in the large color space and adjust the color's saturation and brightness.
- The last option is to drag your cursor to your launched picture if you have the color picker option open. Your pointer will transform into an eyedropper as a result of this action. Finally, change the color underneath your pointer by selecting any place on the image.

Color

How to Work With Brushes

There are many brush tool capabilities accessible in Adobe's colors departments, which are listed below:

1. To use the Brush tool, go to the **Tools area** and choose **Brush** from the drop-down menu.
2. Change the Brush tool's intensity and size while in the settings area. **Note: Users can further decide to choose a different brush top to alter the display of the brush.**
3. Holding the right-hand bracket button several times is a great method to increase the brush tool size.
4. Meanwhile, press and hold the left bracket button several times to decrease the brush tool's size.

How Do You Fine-tune a Selection in Adobe Photoshop

To fine-tune a selection in the mask and select area, use the following methods:

1. Users can use a selection tool, like the Quick selection tool, to make a selection.

2. To kick start the area, activate the options section and tap Select and Mask.
3. Select any view options, such as Overlay, from the View space on the right-hand side of the area. **Note: If you do so, it will give a much more accurate view of your choice.**
4. In the Overlay view, the selected area appears perfect, while the part that is not selected appears red.
5. Select the Brush tool from the Tools section. **Note: This particular tool permits users to paint on a photo that will be included in the chosen workspace.** If you want to remove a workspace, simply hold Option for Mac users and Alt for Windows users while painting on the area you want to remove.
6. Access the Output Settings and Output menu by navigating below to the right-hand side of the area. Then choose Selection, which will be used as the Output.
7. When you're finished, select OK to exit the **Mask and Select area.**

NINE

How Can I Get Rid of Large Objects?

To erase large objects, rather than using the spot healing brush tool, the content-aware fill command is ideal and recommended.

To remove large items, use these steps:

1. Go to the **Layers section** and select the layer with the large items or objects you want to delete.
2. Before removing an object, try to use the selection tool to pick it out. Make sure to include a small background around the object during this step.

3. Tap **Edit and Fill** from the menu section.
4. Select Content-aware and then OK while still in the Fill option. Wait for the Selection to be perfected, as well as the material that fits the backdrop. **Note: A few users can decide to select to hide an item you don't want from the view.**
5. Meanwhile, if you're not happy with the results, try using the content-aware fill tool again. **Note: While trying, you have the opportunity of getting diverse results.**

How to Remove Small Objects

The spot healing brush is especially designed for eliminating small things.

While using the spot healing brush, follow the steps below for deleting small objects:

1. Select the layer containing the little items you want to delete or remove from the Layers menu.
2. Select the Spot Healing Brush tool from the Tools menu.
3. Modify the intensity/rigidity and size of the Spot Healing Brush tool while in the settings area to perfect the object you wish to remove.

4. Finally, choose a little item to erase.

How Can I Change the Saturation and Hue?

The following methods may be used to alter color saturation and hue:

1. Select the picture from the menu option.
2. Then, before choosing Saturation or Hue, go to the Adjustments section.

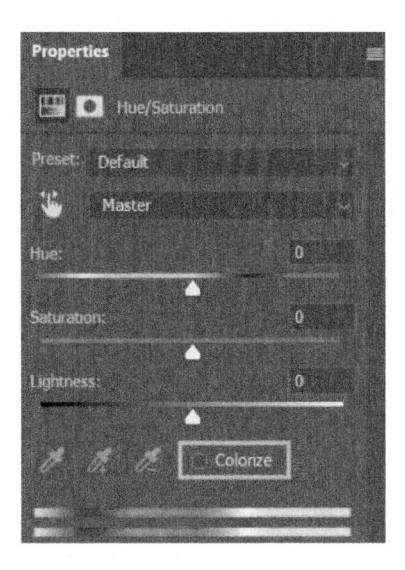

3. Change the Saturation, Lightness, and Hue areas to explore your text.

4. In addition, your changes will be applied to all colors in the pictures provided. The Hue option also changes the colors of a picture. The Saturation option, on the other hand, influences the color concentration in a photograph. Finally, the Lightness option influences the color brightness of a photograph.
5. To use the sliders to alter the hue or saturation of a certain color, open the menu on the top left-hand side of the Hue or Saturation box and choose a color range, such as Yellows. After that, you may play about with the Saturation, Lightness, and Hue settings. Additionally, changes will be made to the selected color range as well as the areas where the color is shown.
6. Finally, click OK to preserve your modifications.

TEN

Selection Basics

A selection isolates a portion of a photograph, enabling you to concentrate on that area without affecting the other pictures. Selections may also be used to alter a portion of a picture without affecting the rest of the image.

Learn all there is to know about Selection by reading the following:

1. Select the Rectangular Marquee tool from the Tools section when it appears. Then, on the photo's face, move your rectangle selection. **Note: The space in the animated border signifies and denotes**

your selection.
2. To add to these, just choose the Add to your choice option. **Note: The icon is found in the choices spot and you may also move it by selecting Shift and moving it.**
3. To decrease the choices you've chosen, click the minus symbol in the options box, or press Option on a Mac or Alt on a Windows computer.
4. You may alter the layer you wish to update at any moment. You may then select whether or not to make certain modifications. Select Image and Adjustments to do so.
5. If your option is selected, the modifications will be applied to the layer's selected space. In the meanwhile, if you copy, edit, filter, paint, or fill, similar things will happen.
6. Once you've finished, touch Select and Deselect to untick the boxes. (On the other hand, you can untick by pressing Command + D on a Mac or Control + D on a PC.)

How to Work With Lasso Tools

The Lasso tools may be used for a variety of purposes, which are mentioned below:

1. Select the Lasso tool from the Tools menu. **Note: The Lasso tool is great for erasing or removing a selected option that you started with another tool.** Simply put, you may utilize the Lasso tool to delete or remove the previously chosen choice.
2. Hold Shift and navigate around the area you wish to include if you want to add more selections made with any tool.
3. In the choices area, choose to Subtract from selected choice to subtract or subtract from a choice. Alternatively, you may navigate about the space you'll be minus by pressing and holding Option on a Mac or Alt on a Windows computer.
4. To delete the previously inserted Selection, press Command + D for Mac users and Control + D for Windows users.

Quick Selection: How to Use It

Follow the steps below to learn how to utilize the quick selection tool:

1. Select the Quick Selection tool from the Tools menu.
2. To select or open a tool, move your cursor to the top of a space.
3. The fast selection tool tries to find picture corners and then immediately stops the selection.
4. After you've made your initial pick, the fast selection tool will immediately shift to the **"Add to Selection"** option.
5. If you need more room, just place it on top of other areas.
6. To narrow down your options, press and hold the Options button on a Mac or the Alt button on a PC while dragging your mouse over the top of other spots to remove them from the list.
7. Change the strength and size of the **Quick Selection tool** in the settings area to test or explore.

How to Flip an Image in Photoshop to Get the Mirror Image of Any Photo

Mirror selfies may be edgy and creative, but they should be approached with caution: you'll need to flip the picture before publishing it if you want any letters or symbols to look as they should in a mirror-taken self portrait.

Fortunately, Photoshop makes it simple to produce a mirror copy of your mirror photos, ensuring that your selfies correctly convey your message.

To do so, follow these three basic steps:

1. Pick **"Open"** in Photoshop CC 2020, then select the file you wish to flip.

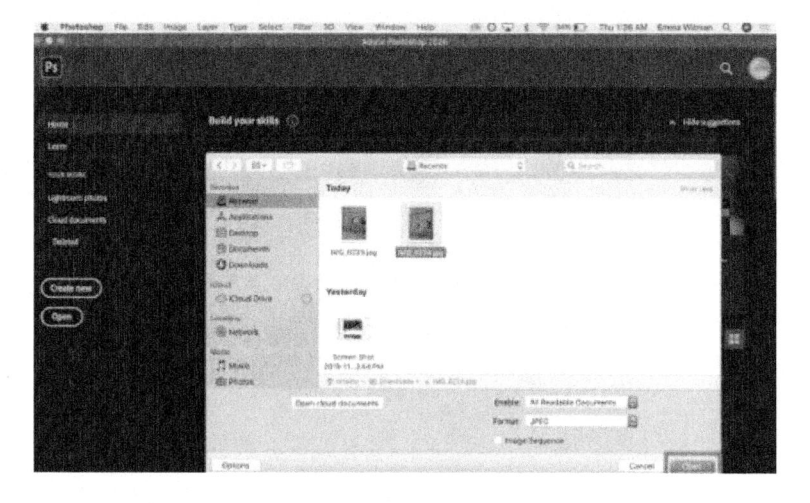

2. From the main toolbar at the top, pick "Image," then scroll down to "Image Rotation," and then select **"Flip Canvas Horizontal."**

3. You'll want to save your flipped picture at this point. Return to "File," then "Save As..." and pick the same name to replace the non-flipped version if you no longer require it, or a new name to save both flipped and non-flipped versions.

Selection Basics

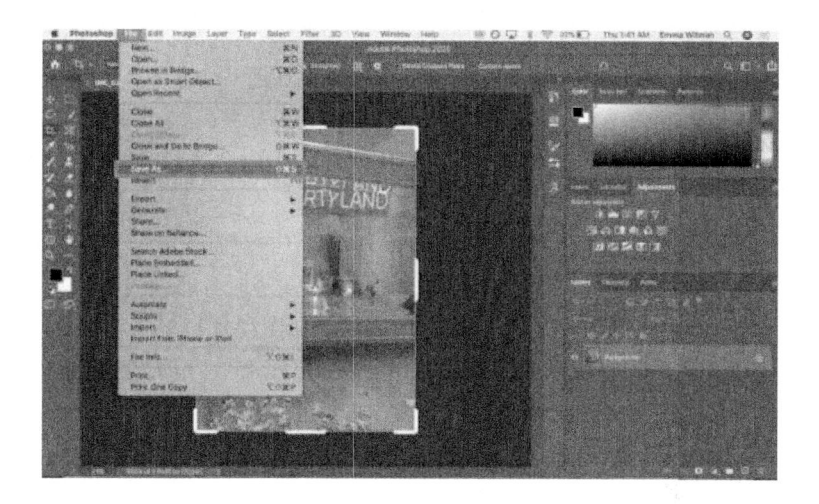

ELEVEN

How Unlock the Background Layer

In certain cases, you may find that your background layer is frozen, leaving you unsure of what to do and what not to do. There are a few different approaches to unlocking the background layers in Adobe.

To unlock the background layer, follow the instructions below:

1. You won't be able to move objects in the document window if the background layer is locked. Users will not, in reality, rearrange things in the layers section. **Note: Also, some editing options will not work like you need to because of the unlocking**

feature.

2. To change the background layer to a regular layer, just click the lock symbol in the layers section next to the layer name's right-hand size.

How Can I Alter the Brightness of a Color?

Users may alter the color of any picture or piece of information they're working on. These modifications may be made in a short amount of time, stored, and even shared with friends and family.

The following are the steps of changing color vibrancy:

1. Select Image from the menu choices, then Adjustments, and lastly Vibrance.
2. You may experiment with different settings by adjusting the sliders. The following is how it works: The Vibrance element modifies the severity of the colors. It also has the most difficult impact on subdued colors in a photograph. The Saturation area, on the other hand, increases the photo's color harshness.

3. Once you've finished adjusting the color's brightness as described above, simply choose OK.

What Is the Significance of Layers?

Layers are essential because they provide users with various functionalities. Layers, for example, may be modified according to the user's preferences. Look at the following examples to understand why layers are important:

1. Layers are essential since the layers section is where they are put up and arranged in a heap. **Note: This is mostly seen in the lower right-hand side of the workspace.** If the layers are not visible, just choose Windows and then Layers.

2. Before making changes to a layer, users must first select one. Simply choose a single item on the right-hand side of the layer's name while in the layers area to select a specific layer. If you want to add additional layers to the ones you've already selected, just hold Command (Mac) or Control (Windows) while choosing new layers.

3. Layers are essential because they mix text, objects, and pictures to create a layered file. Layers allow you to edit, interact with, and move objects onto one another without affecting the remainder of the layer's contents.
4. Select the eye symbol on the left-hand side of the layer in the layers area (**NB: This option will keep the content or File far away from other users**). To display the content, choose once more in a similar location (**NB: This is a perfect way to recall yourself on a specific layer**).

How to Alter the Size of a Layer

If you decide on a layer size and then change your mind, you can easily go back and change it to your desired size. This is a simple procedure that only takes a few steps to complete.

To alter the size of a layer, follow the instructions below:

1. Select single or more layers containing pictures or objects you wish to alter in the Layers area. **Note: This is where you are allowed to choose the image you want to change.**

How to Unlock the Background Layer

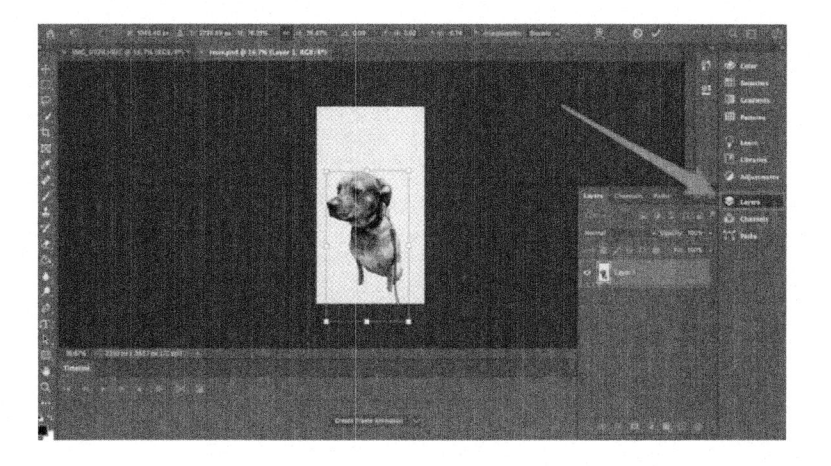

2. Select edit and the **"Free Transform"** option from the drop-down menu. A transform border will appear on your device's screen and around the object you've selected after you've done so.
3. Hold down the Shift key for a few seconds to keep the selected object from changing. You may also adjust the borders until you've found or achieved your ideal size.
4. Drag the object around the picture by moving inside the inner portion of the transform border. Additionally, drag the selected object outside the transform boundary.

Adobe Photoshop for Beginners

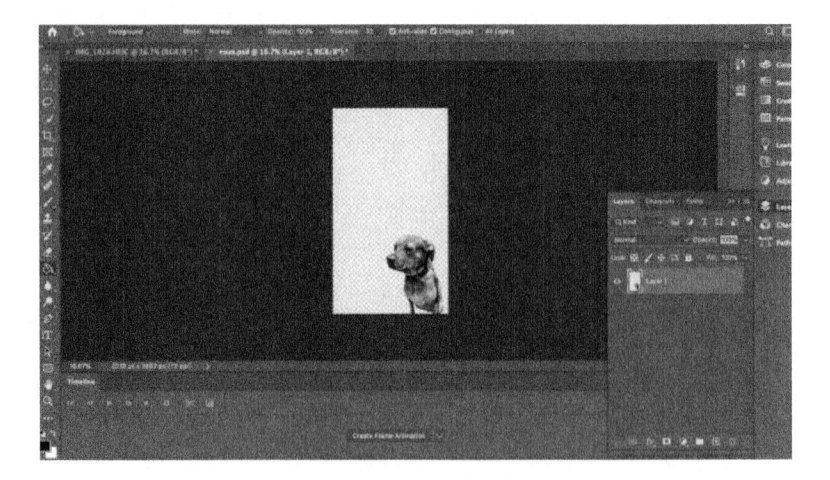

5. Finally, for Windows users, just press Enter to preserve the changes to the layer sizes. Mac users, on the other hand, are required to choose **Return**. Note: For all users, they can choose to select the checkmark located in the options section.

TWELVE

How to Include Pictures into a Layer Design

Additional pictures may be added to a design by users. You should also be aware that each photograph has many layers.

Follow the steps below to effectively add pictures to your layer design:

1. Choose File and then **"Place Embedded"** from the drop-down menu.
2. Go to any picture file and double-click it. Depending on the computer system you're using, image files are different. Users of Macs should choose Finder, while Windows users

should use File Explorer. Finally, decide on a location.
3. Hold down the Shift key for a few seconds to keep the photo's size from altering. Move the picture border's borders to alter the size of the image you've chosen.
4. You can also drag the inner border to position the chosen picture where you want it.
5. Finally, under the choices area, choose the checkmark to finalize the addition. **Note: This option will automatically make a new layer with the selected image.**

How Can I Adjust the Contrast and Brightness?

Depending on when you wish to modify it, you may adjust the brightness and contrast at any moment.

Examine the following options for adjusting brightness and contrast:

1. Select Image from the menu section, then Adjustments, and lastly Brightness and Contrast.

How to Include Pictures into a Layer Design

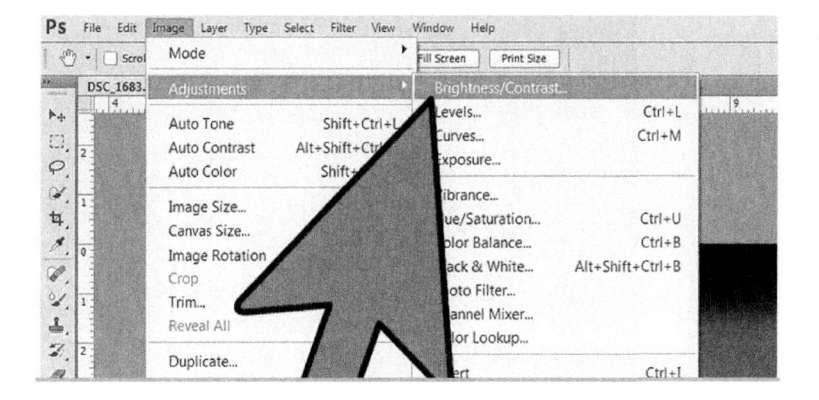

2. Alter the brightness or color intensity of a chosen picture by changing the brightness option. Also, choose whether to increase or decrease the picture contrast by selecting the contrast option.

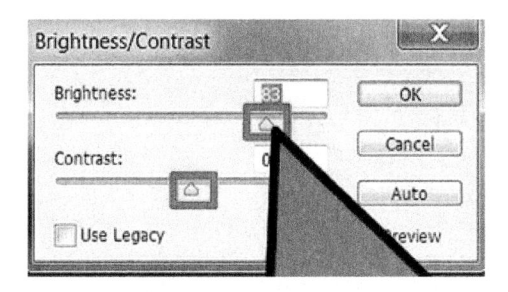

3. When you're finished, click OK. **Note: Selecting OK will mean that the changes will be shown on the chosen layer.**

How Do I Make a Resolution?

Every photograph has a resolution that describes how the picture is shown or displayed to you. Users, on the other hand, have the option of changing the resolution of any picture they don't like.

Changing a photo's resolution will only change its appearance and interior properties.

To discover how to change the resolution of any picture, follow the instructions below:

1. Choose a picture and its size. When a picture is printed on a hardcopy rather than a softcopy, the image resolution in this area simply refers to the number of photo pixels supplied to every inch.

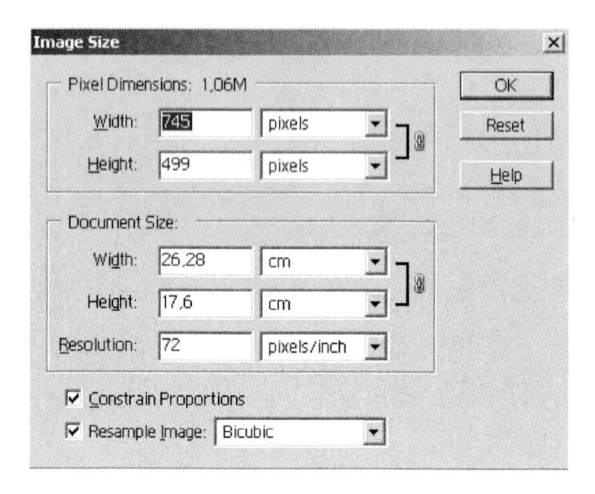

```
Image Size                                          ×
 ┌ Pixel Dimensions: 1,06M ──────────────┐    ┌─────────┐
                                              │   OK    │
     Width:  [745]     pixels      ▼  ┐       └─────────┘
                                       ⑧      ┌─────────┐
    Height:  499      pixels      ▼  ┘       │  Reset  │
                                              └─────────┘
 └───────────────────────────────────────┘    ┌─────────┐
                                              │  Help   │
 ┌ Document Size: ───────────────────────┐    └─────────┘
     Width:  26,28    cm          ▼  ┐
                                       ⑧
    Height:  17,6     cm          ▼  ┘
 Resolution:  72      pixels/inch  ▼
 └───────────────────────────────────────┘

    ☑ Constrain Proportions
    ☑ Resample Image: [ Bicubic     ▼ ]
```

How to Include Pictures into a Layer Design

2. You may opt not to modify the height and width anytime you want to print, depending on what you think is appropriate. **Note: If you leave it untouched, Adobe will automatically set the inches to printable size or version.**

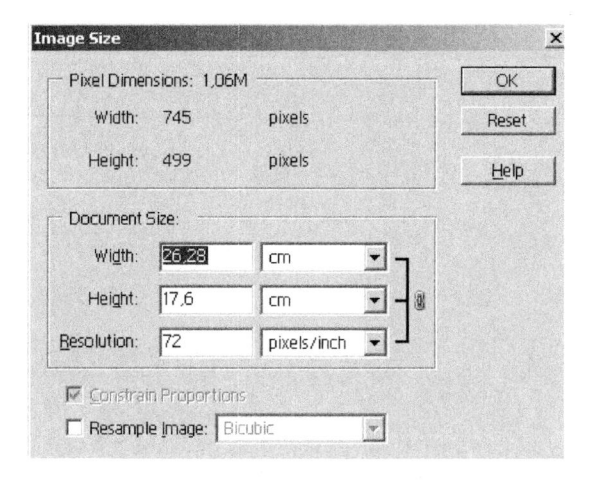

3. To retain the initial picture pixel number, untick the Resample option. **Note: Ensure you do this if you still want to have the first photo pixel number before it was changed.**

Adobe Photoshop for Beginners

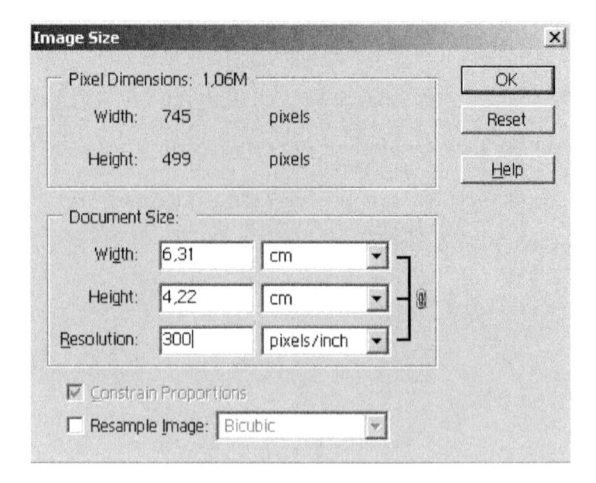

4. Proceed to the resolution section and choose the amount of pixels you want for each inch. If you wish to print a hardcopy, the right quantity to select is 300. **Note: Once done, it will alter the number of inches in the height and width sections.**
5. Finally, click OK to complete your changes and save them.

How to Crop and Straighten a Picture

Adobe users may utilize the crop option to straighten and crop a picture. Cropping a photograph entails decreasing its size and removing the image's undesirable areas.

Straightening a picture is similar to cropping a photo, and the two may be done in the same area. To straighten and crop a picture, follow the instructions below:

1. In the tools box, go to the **Crop section. Note: Once you tap on the Crop tool, a crop border will be displayed on your device screen.**
2. Change the form and size of the crop border by moving any corner.

3. Also, carefully and strategically position the picture in the crop border by moving inside the crop border.

Adobe Photoshop for Beginners

4. Go outside the crop boundary to straighten or alter the size and appearance of the picture. **Note: Carry out the straitening and cropping of photos in this option before saving your changes.**
5. Finally, press Enter if you're using Windows. Mac users, on the other hand, should choose Return to complete and save their cropped picture. **Note: Otherwise, from the options section, you can select the checkmark to end your cropping changes and save it.**

THIRTEEN

How Can I Change the Size of the Canvas?

On Adobe Photoshop, you may add additional spaces to the document canvas.

To change the canvas size, follow the instructions below:

1. Choose a picture and then a canvas size.

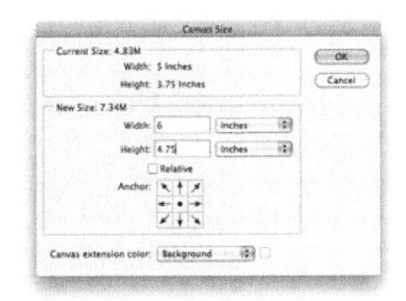

2. If you'd like to add a canvas, provide the desired height and width.
3. In the Width and Height text boxes, type in new values. Using the pop-up options, you may easily alter the unit of measurement. To define an amount of space for Photoshop to add or subtract around your picture, tick the Relative check box. When you're adding or removing equal amounts of canvas around images with fractional measurements, this feature comes in handy.
4. Indicate where you want the anchor to go. The anchor depicts how the picture is positioned inside the canvas. Photoshop automatically centers the image and adds or removes the canvas around it by default. To asymmetrically add or remove the canvas surrounding the picture, click any of the other eight squares.
5. When you lower the Width or Height setting and then click OK, a warning box displays, asking if you're sure you want to continue since the picture will be clipped. This is another method of cropping a picture, albeit not one

you'll use on a regular basis.

6. Click OK after selecting your canvas color from the Canvas extension color pop-up menu. Select Foreground, Background, White, Black, Gray, or Other from the drop-down menu. If you choose Other, Photoshop will take you to the Color Picker, where you may choose any color. The current backdrop color is shown via the little swatch to the right of the pop-up menu. You may also use the Color Picker by clicking this swatch.

Tips and Tricks to Using Adobe Photoshop

If you're new to Adobe Photoshop, the sheer quantity of panels, icons, and tools on the screen may be overwhelming. Adobe develops some of the most powerful and complex applications available, giving you a wide range of choices. It does, however, provide a high learning curve, with a lot to practice and learn. Here are some Photoshop hints and tips to help you get the most out of your time with the program.

Choose Colors from Anywhere

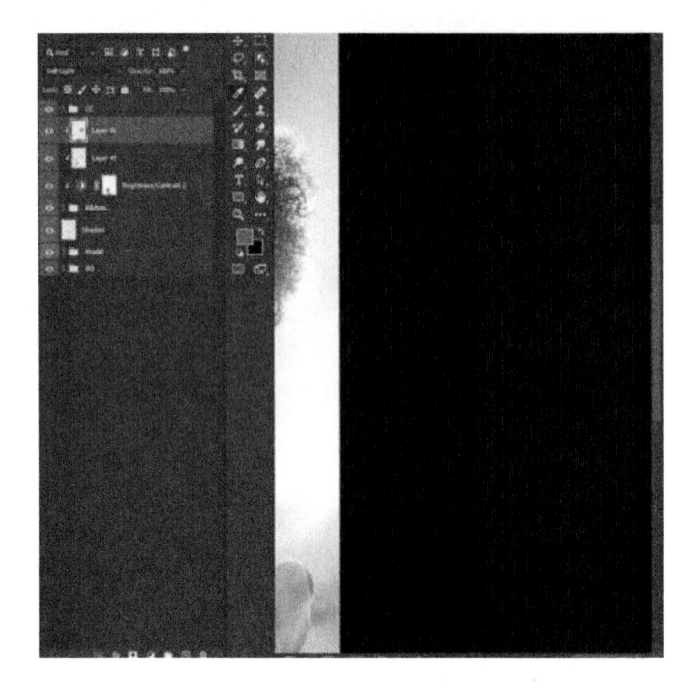

Stop taking screenshots of stuff simply to get the colors! Simply use the Eye Dropper tool, minimize Photoshop, drop the dropper onto your canvas, and move anywhere outside of Photoshop.

Install Custom Photoshop Brushes

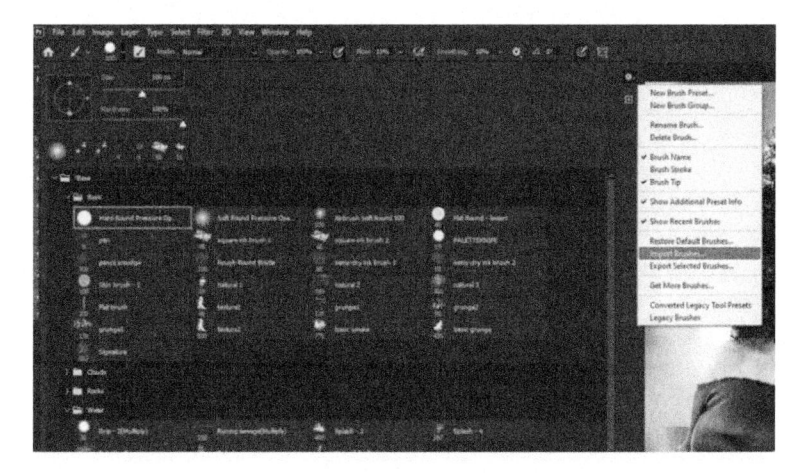

Don't limit yourself to the Photoshop brushes that come pre-installed. Go into your bushes, click the Gear button, and choose Import Brushes to try out one of the hundreds of brushes available on the internet.

What Is the Best Way to Make a Rain Texture?

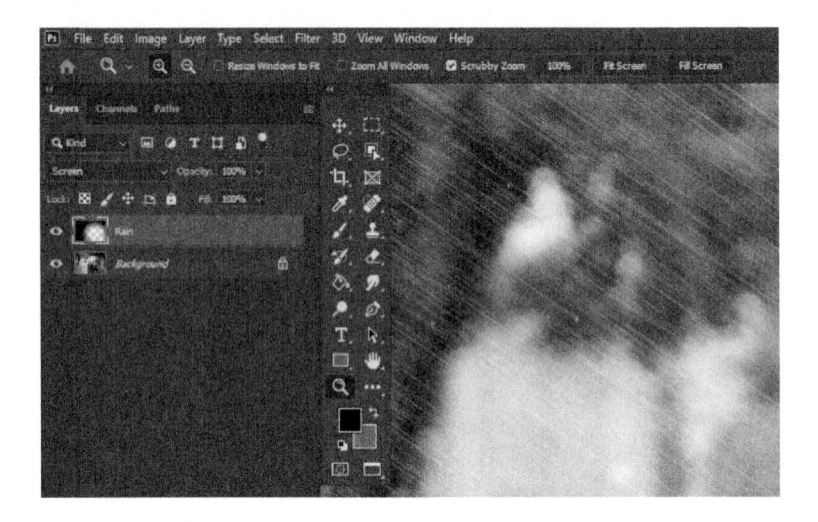

Raindrops falling from the sky are a terrific way to add drama to your photos, but nature doesn't always cooperate. Create your own rain by starting with a dark layer, adding some Noise, then a slanted Motion Blur, and lastly setting the layer to Screen! With a little contrast, you've got instant rain.

Create a Light Bleed Effect in a Flash

Create a new layer and paint white towards the top of your picture with a large fluffy white brush to provide a slight light bleed to help merge any image. Reduce the layer's opacity to finish it off.

Use Blend If

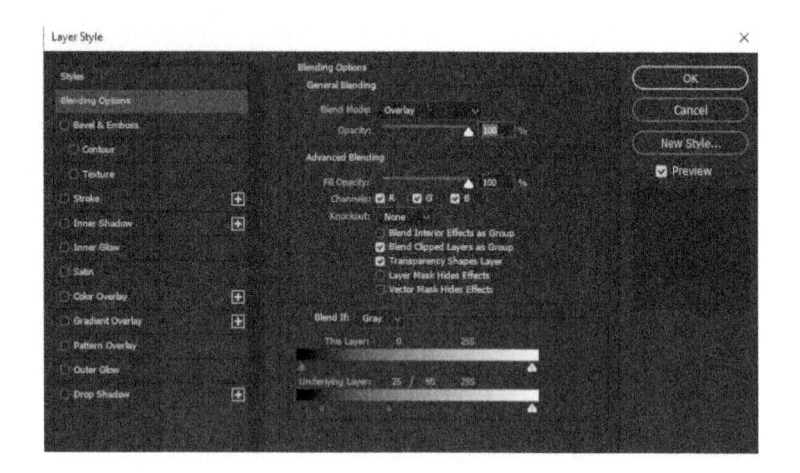

By double-clicking the layer you'd want to blend, scrolling down to Blend If, then fiddling with the sliders while holding Shift, you can blend anything onto everything! The uppermost layer will begin to merge with the ones underneath it.

How to Quickly Copy Layer Styles

Do you have a layer style that you'd want to apply to a number of additional layers? Drag the FX symbol from the original layer to the target layers while holding down the Alt key. There will be no need to tinker with settings since the layer styles will be applied immediately.

How to Make Text Have Multiple Stroke Effects

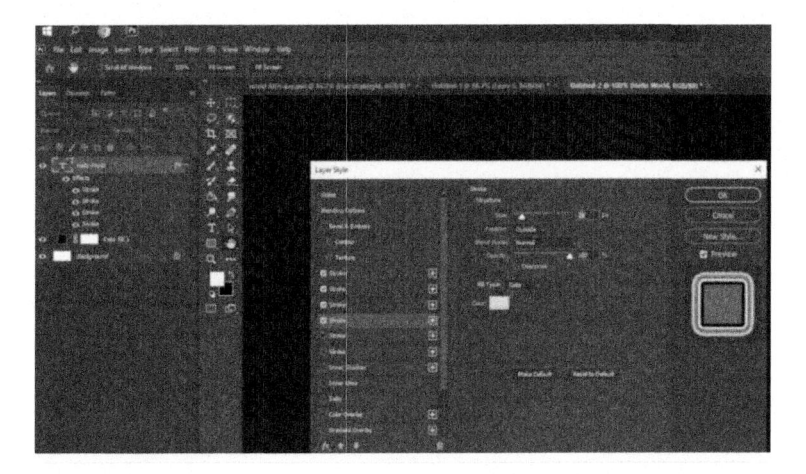

Why limit yourself to one line stroke when you may have two? To add a Stroke layer effect to the text layer, double-click it. To add another Stroke, press the Plus button. You may add as many as you like.

Adobe Photoshop for Beginners

Learn How to Use Keyboard Shortcuts

Keyboard/Mouse Shortcut	Action
Ctrl + Alt/Option (PC/Mac) + 0	100% Magnification
Ctrl + 0	Fit Screen
Ctrl + Spacebar	Temporarily select the Zoom tool (Zoom in)
Ctrl + Alt/Option (PC/Mac) + Spacebar	Temporarily select the Zoom tool (Zoom out)
Spacebar	Temporarily select the Hand tool
Tab	Hide the Tool bar and Panels
Shift + Tab	Hide the Panels but keep the Tools
Page Up or Page Down	Scroll Up or Scroll Down the area contained within the screen
Shift + Page Up or Page Down	Scroll Up or Scroll Down in 10 units
Double Click on the Zoom tool icon	100% Magnification
Double Click on the Hand tool icon	Fit Screen

Thanks to a variety of helpful keyboard shortcuts, experienced Photoshop users can alter images fast and simply. It's easier to master shortcuts for the activities you're most likely to do often than it is to navigate through dropdown menus and submenus (which may seem particularly complex when new Photoshop upgrades are released).

Learn to Merge Shapes

Select your shape layers and then Right-Click > Merge Forms to generate rapid custom shapes using the shapes you've previously produced. Bam! Multiple forms have now merged into one.

Make Destructive Changes to New Layers At All Times

If you're familiar with Lightroom, you've already spent time making non-destructive changes. Adjustment layers in Lightroom, in essence, do not alter the images themselves. Because the changes are saved as a distinct file, you can always go back to the original picture without causing any damage.

Photoshop may also be used in this manner if your file and workspace are properly prepared. When you open a picture, the Background layer will display. Make a duplicate of the picture using Layer > New > Layer from Background to preserve it intact and unmodified.

On top of the Background layer, an exact duplicate of your background layer will appear. You may now change your background copy as much as you like while still having access to the original version.

For future editing, make sure you save your Photoshop files appropriately.

Even the most skilled retouchers may sometimes flatten an image's layers and save it in the incorrect format. When you just have a flattened jpeg to work with and want to change one small element of your project, it may be very irritating.

Save a PSD file of your most complex editing work to prevent future hassles. PSD files save your layers separately so you may go back to them at any moment to make changes to your photos.

It's worth noting that PSD files take up more space on your hard disk than compressed JPG files, so make sure you have enough space. If you need extra storage capacity, it's simple to update your internal hard drive and much simpler to add an external portable disk.

Experiment With Layer Masks

Layer masks are one of Photoshop's most powerful features. You can use masks to conceal any part of a layer, and you may apply them to as many layers as you like.

For example, if you're altering a portrait and want to brighten the eyes, you may use a layer mask to pick only the regions you want to brighten. If you wish to lighten the shadows on the face, you may do it using a second layer mask. Add more layer masks to darken the backdrop or change the color of the hair. The possibilities are endless.

Mask editing is one of the most essential Photoshop abilities to master because of its versatility and reversibility. The sooner you master them, the more fluid your editing sessions will become.

Find Out What Works Best for You and Stick to It

It's essential to note that with Photoshop, there are many methods to accomplish the same outcomes. There is no one-size-fits-all approach to picture editing. Although video tutorials may teach you several methods for achieving the same look, the ideal choice is the one that you can repeat with ease.

Using Photoshop to Warp Text

Look at the top-right of the Type Tool's toolbar with your text layer selected and the Type Tool active. You'll see a "T" symbol with a curved line below it. To view a variety of built-in text arcs and bends, click that button.

How to Create a Photoshop Frequency Separation Action

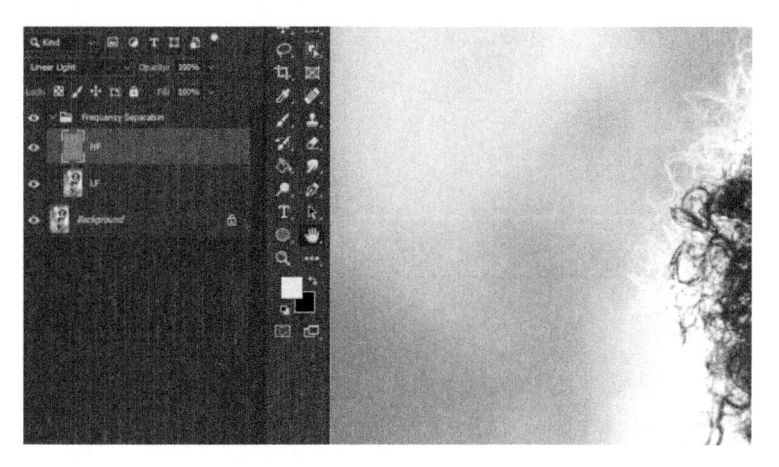

Do you ever wonder how models get their flawless high-fashion skin? It's referred to as frequency separation. Make two layers with your picture, one with a Gaussian Blur and the other with a High Pass filter. Linear Light should be selected. Fix the color and skin tone with the blurred layer, and the texture with the high pass layer.

How to Make a Smart Object

When you bring a layer into Photoshop, it immediately becomes a Smart Object, but did you know you can convert any layer into a Smart Object? By right-clicking the layer and selecting Convert to Smart Object, you can begin utilizing this non-destructive editing powerhouse.

Photoshop Brushes: How to Make One

Did you know that you can make a custom-made brush out of any black and white image? Crop the picture or item as tiny as possible after it's greyscaled, then go to Edit > Define Brush Preset.

conclusion

Adobe Photoshop is regarded as one of the finest photo editing applications in the world. It comes with a variety of interesting tools and other top-notch features that will make your editing procedure simple and painless.

It's almost likely that you've begun your editing adventure with Adobe Photoshop after reading this user guide. Instead of pondering and giving up quickly, critically examine our user guide, and you'll be an expert in no time.

Also, you may run into any problems when using the program; just refer to this user guide to clear up any confusion. Finally, this book covers all you need to know about generating new pictures, editing, retouching, and revamping existing photos to make them seem fresh and new.

Every book project I write is meant to pass across information and educate the general public, and that is why I am pleased with every person that purchases my book.

Not a single individual buyer is exempted from my good book and they also encourage me to publish more exciting books. What motivate me the more is the positive 5 star reviews commented by my readers, which also increase the book's visibility. You are all special people.

Leaving a comment means leaving me with something to hold onto. I would reckon and indulge you to always visit the review section and leave something you think will improve my writing and book, especially in subsequent ones to come.

I never take your reviews for granted and I'm committed to serving you with the best.

Thanks!

Printed in Great Britain
by Amazon